Words have power! Stories and metaphors told wisely can influence perception, make new meaning and deeply change lives. Inspired by the power of metaphor, visualization and hypnotic languaging to bring about generative change, this book provides a set of *m*BIT (multiple Brain Integration Techniques) and NLP inspired guided-visualization and relaxation scripts that you can read out loud to lead the people you love into deep and generative trances. The scripts in this book provide beautiful journeys deep into mountains, forests and beaches; filling you, and those you are reading them to, with the sensory experiences of gliding and travelling through these beautiful, restful and spiritual places.

Research shows that visualization is almost as powerful as the real experience. And not everyone is skilled at creating metaphors and guided visualizations impromptu. This book therefore teaches you the science behind the Journeys, shows you how to read them, and provides the scripts to make it easy to guide someone into a deep journey of entrancing delight.

mBIT Guided Journeys for the Heart, Mind & Soul

Grant Soosalu

www.mbraining.com

First Published 2018
TimeBinding Publications

Contents

_m_ BIT Guided
Journeys
Roadmap

Meta-Journeys - The Journey towards these Journeys

Nearly 40 years ago, having just learned NLP (Neuro Linguistic Programming), I was inspired by the power of metaphor, visualization and hypnotic languaging to bring about generative change. I decided I wanted to create a set of NLP based guided-visualization scripts that could be read out loud to lead people into deep and generative trances. To do this, I spent time walking in the Australian mountains, forests and beaches with pen and paper, documenting the sensory experiences of gliding and travelling through these beautiful, restful and spiritual places. The written notes of these journeys formed the basis for the scripts in this book.

More recently as the main co-developer of *m*BIT (multiple Brain Integration Techniques), and with deep insights from the field of cognitive linguistics and embodied cognition, I decided to revisit the scripts and add in the much deeper *m*BIT and neuroscience informed insights into them. So that, what you now have in your hands are a set of powerful guided-visualization scripts you can use to either facilitate yourself or others into deeply integrative, relaxing and generative trance-like states that will help bring the human spirit alive.

The Power of Words

"Language is the means by which we organize and shape our experience"

Dr. Annabelle Lukin

"Our language influences our perceptions"

Prof. Peter Senge

Words have power! As linguistic beings, it is largely through language that we create our reality. Stories and metaphors told wisely can influence perception, make new meaning and deeply change lives. As beautifully articulated by the great and sage storyteller himself, Prof. Joseph Campbell (1991), in his work on myth and story and its power to influence human experience:

"You are the hero of your own story... The prime function of mythology and rite is to supply the symbols that carry the human spirit forward."

Prof. Joseph Campbell

And adding to this, in their insightful text on cognitive linguistics, Professors Mark Johnson and George Lakoff (1980), show that much of metaphor is deeply embodied. Stories therefore impact us in both body and mind, and as we'll see from the scientific insights of the new field of *m*BIT (multiple Brain Integration Techniques), our words can influence us at the heart, gut and autonomic levels.

*m*BIT (multiple Brain Integration Techniques)

*m*BIT is a fascinating new coaching, leadership and personal evolution methodology for liberating the human spirit. It is based on recent Neuroscience discoveries that we have complex, adaptive and functional neural networks, or *'brains'*, in our heart and gut regions. These brains have their own domains of expertise and competencies and this explains why we all sense the importance of gut instinct or gut intuition in our lives and how our heart is a source of important intuitive intelligence and feeling. Research in the field of *m*BIT has found that wise decisions require alignment of our multiple brains (head, heart and gut) and that unless you tap into the intuitive intelligence of the heart and gut, your decisions and their results can lead to serious issues for your health, happiness and the quality of your life. You can read more about *m*BIT in the Appendix or go to www.mbraining.com to find out more about my book, co-authored with Marvin Oka, called '*mBraining — Using your Multiple Brains to do Cool Stuff!*'

The science behind *m*BIT

To understand the power of using *m*BIT in guided creative-visualizations, it helps to more deeply review the work and evidence for the '*multiple brains*'. Though if you are already trained in *m*BIT and in particular if you've completed *m*BIT Master Coach Certification, then you can skip over this section.

As you'll know from above, over the last decade or so, the field of neuroscience has uncovered that we have complex, adaptive and functional neural intelligences or '*brains*' in various regions of the body. These brains have been shown to be deeply involved in what is called embodied cognition (Park & Thayer, 2014; Craig, 2014; Critchley, 2015). For example, scientists in the new fields of Neuro-cardiology (Armour, 2007; Thayer, 2007) and Neuro-gastro-enterology (Gershon, 1999; Holzer et al., 2001; Mayer, 2011) have shown that we have brains in the heart and enteric or gut regions and that these neural systems are involved in emotion, decision-making and intuitive wisdom (Berntson, Sarter & Cacioppo, 2003; Holzer, 2017).

Some researchers in the field of Autonomic Neuroscience are also now saying that the Autonomic Nervous System can be seen as a '*brain*' (Howard & Crandall, 2007; Beissner et al., 2013; Mravec & Hulin, 2006) and there is small but growing evidence of a '*sexual, pelvic or reproductive brain*' (Wolf, 2013; Robinson, 1917).

Based on the neuroscience evidence, and utilizing it to inform behavioural modeling and action research, Soosalu and Oka (2012) created the new field of *m*BIT Coaching. *m*BIT provides tools and insights into how to communicate with the multiple brains and tap into and align them for greater levels of intuitive wisdom; and you can imagine how useful and powerful this could be when utilized in guided-visualization processes. The research on *m*BIT has also uncovered that each of our multiple brains has a *'Highest Expression'*. This is the most adaptive and integrative state, that when aligned across brains helps produce an emergence of wisdom.

The highest expressions of the multiple brains:

- The Autonomic Brain – **Coherence and Calmness**

- The Heart Brain – **Compassion**

- The Head Brain – **Creativity**

- The Gut Brain – **Courage**

- The Reproductive/Sex Brain – **Co-creativity**

- The emergent *mBraining* **Wisdom** of all brains working together as one.

So the guided-visualization Journeys in this book are designed to evoke aspects and prime functions of the head, heart, gut, autonomic and pelvic neural intelligences. They also entrain the Journeyer into the Highest Expressions of their multiple brains and encourage the emergence of deeper intuitive wisdom in the person's life. As you read through the Journey scripts, notice the direct, indirect and metaphorical references to each of the brains and the senses and functions that belong with each brain.

Neuro Linguistic Programming

Neuro Linguistic Programming (NLP) is a behavioral technology of change that is focused on the structure of human excellence. It is a profound set of skills and techniques that can be used to bring about transformational change. For a more in-depth summary of some of its models and ideas used in this book, take a look in the Appendix.

Fundamentally however, NLP provides ways of communicating with both the conscious and unconscious minds to influence them in generative ways. These techniques were originally created by behavioral modeling of *'therapeutic wizards'* such as Milton Erickson, Virginia Satir and Fritz Perls.

NLP and En-trance-ing Language

"Hypnosis is nothing but a profoundly compelling imaginal fantasy that can produce deep shifts in consciousness."

Fromm and Shor (2009)

In the field of NLP there is a set of tools and distinctions known as the Milton Model (or sometimes known as Milton Patterns). These linguistic and behavioral patterns were modeled from Milton Erickson and are used to guide people into hypnotic trance. Milton was a noted American psychiatrist and medical hypnotherapist and was considered to be one of the best hypnosis practitioners in the world. He was a wizard at *artfully guiding* people into deeply generative trances to unlock new possibilities in their lives and bring about unconscious change.

Richard Bandler and John Grinder, the co-developers of NLP, modeled Milton's patterns and how he used language to induce and maintain trance in order to contact the hidden resources of the personality (O'Connor & Seymour, 2011). You can read more about the Milton Model in the Appendix, or grab one of Bandler and Grinder's wonderful books listed in the references section, such as Trance-formations (1981), or Patterns of the Hypnotic Techniques of Milton H. Erickson, Volumes 1 and 2 (1976, 1996).

The Milton model has three primary aspects: Building rapport with the person undergoing trance; Overloading and distracting the conscious mind so that unconscious communication can be more easily achieved, and; Allowing for ambiguity in artfully guiding the person to enable their own personal interpretation of the hypnotic communication.

Throughout the Journeys in this book, you will find that Milton patterns have been used extensively to construct the Journey experience and to guide the Journeyer into more deeply relaxing and trance-like states. This includes using patterns such as:

- **Pacing current experience** (e.g. "as you are hearing the sound of my voice…")

- **Ambiguity** (e.g. 'here' vs 'hear')

- **Conjunctions and causal linkages** (e.g. and, as, this allows you, etc.)

- **Cause and Effect** (e.g. "and this allows you to go deeper")

- **Embedded Commands** (e.g. "and you can FIND YOURSELF drifting deeper now")

- **Presuppositions** (e.g. "and you can relax even more now" which presupposes they are already relaxing)

- **Selectional Restriction Violation** (e.g. "as you are sitting now on the meditative rock")

- **Double Bind** (e.g. "you can follow along with the Journey, or not")

- **Metaphor** (e.g. extensive use of symbolic and metaphorical elements such as rainbows, mountains, deep pools etc.)

- **Nested Loops and Layering** (e.g. opening a loop and then returning at the end to the same loop)

- **Submodalities** (e.g. making things brighter, closer, stronger, deeper)

- **Etc.** (see the Appendix for a fuller list of Milton Patterns).

Influencing the Unconscious Mind

"The conscious mind determines the actions, the unconscious mind determines the reactions; and the reactions are just as important as the actions."

E. Stanley Jones

Trance is a state of human consciousness involving focused attention, reduced peripheral awareness and an altered state of mind. In essence it involves shifting from a *'normal'* state of consciousness to an altered state that makes parts of the unconscious mind more accessible. As you will learn in the Appendix, in the section on NLP, in the field of Psychology there is still active and ongoing debate about the unconscious mind, its role, existence and structure. In NLP, however, there is an accepted model of the unconscious mind that is largely ratified by recent research in Cognitive Psychology (e.g. see Bargh & Morsella, 2008).

In NLP, the unconscious mind is seen as all of those processes that occur in the brain outside of consciousness. That is, the unconscious mind can be thought of as the *'other-than-conscious'* mind. These are the processes for example that are responsible for brain and body functioning, for performing visual processing, and for unconsciously directing attention and awareness. Thousands and thousands of both simple and complex processes and patterns, operating generally outside of your conscious awareness.

And as the field of *m*BIT shows, much of the intuitive intelligence of the heart and gut brains is processed out of our conscious awareness. So we form unconscious patterns and habits in how we communicate with and tune into the wisdom of our heart and gut and how they respond to the world. What's fascinating is that there is growing evidence that hypnosis and trance allow us to shift into a state of consciousness that is more heart and gut based and connected.

The Australian psychiatrist and hypnotherapist, Dr. Ainslie Meares (1960; 1970) pioneered a method of guided hypnosis and meditation that he believed allowed people to access a more primitive (in evolutionary terms), regressed and atavistic state. Meares was an internationally recognized expert in the medical uses of hypnotism and in the early 1960's travelled the world researching therapeutic trance phenomenon exhibited by yogis, lamas, witch-doctors and aboriginal healers (Meares, 1973). What he found is that under trance, the higher (more evolved) conscious functions of a person's brain become switched off, and the person reverts to a far more archaic and embodied mental state. In this state, cognitive processing is significantly altered so that suggestions are more readily accepted without any of the normal cognitive filters and verifications interfering in the process.

After years of research and clinical application, Meares came to believe that it was this atavistic regression rather than the hypnotic treatments that helped the patient. He concluded that the regression enabled the mind to rest and restored its equilibrium in a way that was analogous to recuperative sleep.

"It is in the stillness of our own self that we can learn those things that escape us in the noise of the market place..."

Dr Ainslie Meares

Meares' insights are nicely backed up by recent research on the neural basis of hypnosis. Studies have found that when in trance, subjects increase the connectivity and activity between the prefrontal cortex and an area deep inside the brain called the insula (Jiang et al., 2017; Li et al., 2018; Oakley & Halligan, 2009). The insula is involved in what is called embodied interoceptive awareness or in other words, your sense of deep inner connection with the Autonomic Nervous System, your heart brain and your gut brain. The insula represents your inner somatic knowing. So under hypnosis, your state of consciousness shifts from your normal self-conscious cognitive state to a more deeply and primitive embodied state. You get access to a focused attention on your deeper intuitive intelligence.

"Until you make the unconscious conscious, it will direct your life and you will call it fate."

C.G. Jung

So the Journeys in this book are designed to evoke the processes of embodied mental ataraxis that Meares pioneered and to produce

16

relaxed trance-like states that open you up to the deeper inner you. And from an *m*BIT perspective, this allows your inner wisdom to emerge, making each Journey a very generative and regenerative process. By bringing the unconscious intuitive wisdom to consciousness – each journey provides a gift, message, dream or guidance to emerge deeper wisdom from the unconscious intuitions of heart, head, gut and Autonomic intelligences and to thereby help you create generative change in your life.

The Power of Visualization

"Guided imagery is one of the most potent tools we have as individuals to manage stress, unleash our creativity, change our attitudes, set and reach goals, tap into our inner wisdom, relax, stimulate peak performance, and activate our natural healing powers."

Andrew E. Schwartz

Visualization and imagery are natural ways the human nervous system stores, accesses and processes information. It is the coding system in which memories, dreams, imagination, fantasies, desires and expectations are stored. It is also a way of thinking and using your multiple brains that evokes both cognitive and embodied sensory experiences and attributes. It is powerful. As Marty Rossman (2006), points out in an article on *'Guided Imagery in Clinical Practice'*: *"In the absence of competing sensory cues, the body tends to respond to imagery as it would to a genuine external sensory stimulus."*

So visualization and imagery have physiological and psychological consequences:

"Physically, imagery has the ability to directly influence the Autonomic Nervous System, and the power of imagination can be recruited to promote specific physiological changes as an aid to healing. In addition, many studies indicate that certain imagery techniques may stimulate physiologic processes including immune, nervous, and endocrine responses which can accelerate the healing process."

Kodeeswara Prabu & Subhash, 2015

Indeed, guided imagery and visualization have been shown in hundreds of studies to affect almost all major physiological control systems, including respiration, heart rate, blood pressure, metabolic rates in cells, gastrointestinal mobility and secretion, sexual function, and even immune responsiveness (Weil, 2018). Guided Imagery has also been used to improve the immune response in cancer patients, to help alleviate depression, for surgery patients before and after surgery to decrease pain, to reduce blood loss during surgery, to reduce menopausal symptoms, and numerous other applications (Micozzi, 2006).

To achieve these results, guided visualization processes use positive imagery such as tranquil nature scenes and relaxing scenarios to bring about a more relaxed, calm and grounded state. In essence it is a form of relaxation therapy that uses imagery to facilitate generative unconscious states that can facilitate resolution of various emotional, physical and psychological issues and problems. For example, guided imagery with progressive muscle relaxation has been found to substantially decrease recurrent abdominal pain in children (Weydert et al., 2006). And guided imagery also has a proven record in stress reduction (Weigensberg et al., 2009), relief of dyspnea and sleep disturbance and beneficial effects on heart related symptoms (Kwekkeboom & Bratzke, 2016).

Visualization is also used extensively in sports, and for good reason. Imagination is almost as powerful as the real thing.

"When you visualize then you materialize.
If you've been there in the mind you'll go there in the body."

Dennis Waitley

For example, if right now you begin to vividly imagine sucking deeply on a sour, tart slice of fresh, tangy lemon; you will likely find you soon begin to salivate naturally. As the great psychologist and personal motivator, Dr Dennis Waitley, found when working with Olympic athletes:

"We took Olympic athletes and had them run their event only in their mind, and then hooked them up to sophisticated biofeedback equipment. Incredibly, the same muscles fired in the same sequence when they were running the race in their mind as when they were running it on the track. How could this be? Because the mind can't distinguish whether you're really doing it or whether it's just a practice. If you've been there in your mind you'll go there in the body." (Waitley, 2002).

There is also growing scientific evidence that shows that imagery and mental training can improve muscle strength (Yao et al., 2013; Shackell & Standing, 2007). In one of the most well-known studies on creative visualization in sports (Scaglione & Cummins, 1993), Russian scientists compared four groups of Olympic athletes in terms of their training schedules. In the first group there was 100% physical training, the other three groups had varying percentages of physical and mental visualization training. The results showed that Group 4, with 75% of their time devoted to mental training, performed the best. Sports psychologists are also saying that visualization helps boost more than strength and performance, but also increases athletes' confidence and ability to ignore distractions (McCormack, 2006).

So you can see why we utilize guided visualization and imagery in our Journeys for the heart, mind and soul. These processes are powerful and bring many benefits. And the repetition of these exercises causes learning and ongoing conditioning effects, so that the positive physical, emotional and psychological changes can eventually become available wherever and whenever the Journeyer chooses to use them. These benefits also accrue for the Guide as much as the Journeyer, since in reading out the scripts the Guide's conscious and unconscious minds are also being deeply influenced by the words and imagery. Also remember, as you'll see when you explore the Journey scripts, imagery isn't necessarily just visual, but uses all of the senses to evoke a full body and mind experience.

Benefits of Guided Imagery

According to the research, some of the many potential benefits that come from the use of visualization and guided imagery include (Naparstek, 2016; Jain et al., 2012; Weydert et al., 2006):

- Reduced anxiety and greater levels of calmness

- Decreased impacts of stress

- Improved management of chronic pain, including gut-based pain

- Deeper and more restorative sleep

- Increased sense of well-being, hope, and optimism

- Greater sense of self-efficacy, personal agency and increased motivation to move forward with goals

- Decreased and less intense depressive episodes

- Better ability to manage emotional reactivity including panic, anger, grief, and discouragement

- Improved relationships with family, co-workers, and friends

- A renewed connection to inner spirituality and a sense of reassurance and comfort that can come with it.

While the guided visualizations and imagery in the Journeys in this book are not being utilized as a therapy technique and therefore not all of the benefits are likely to accrue from their use. Nevertheless, the deep states of relaxation and the generative messages and symbolism in each Journey are likely to provide many useful and powerful benefits. And it is good to be aware of the sorts of changes that can occur.

Possible Contraindications

Please note that while there appears to be little scientific evidence for contraindications to guided visualizations (Kodeeswara Prabu & Subhash, 2015; Naparstek, 2016), nevertheless, it is recommended that caution be exercised and guided visualization processes and relaxation and mindfulness exercises not be delivered to or practiced by those experiencing:

- Paranoid schizophrenia or other forms of psychoses or extreme neuroticism or the like

- Extreme stress or agitation or the like

- Extreme depression or suicidal ideation or the like

- PTSD, anxiety disorders or severe trauma or the like

- Extreme obsessive compulsive disorder or the like

- Proneness to stress-induced asthma attacks

- Any form of severe heart condition such as takotsubo or the like

- Pregnancy

- Any severe psychological or psychiatric condition

As used in the Journeys in this book, it must once again be emphasized that' guided imagery is not being utilized as a therapy model; instead it is a generative educational process. The Guide does not tell the Journeyer what to do – the guide purely provides the gentle means for the Journeyer to discover and experience the intuitive wisdom that exists within themselves.

However, if at any time someone being guided on one of these Journeys begins to experience any untoward or distressing symptoms, you should discontinue the process immediately and help the person come back to a normal and balanced state. Getting them to take a gentle walk, if they are normally able to be mobile, is likely to help them to return to their normal state. Drinking a glass of water may also help. Before using these guided visualization and relaxation Journeys with anyone with the above conditions, please ensure you have permission from their mental health or other primary health care practitioner.

Green Space

There is now a growing body of substantial research that has consistently found that exposure to the natural environment, to bushland, forests, trees and nature – to what is called 'green space' – is positively associated with increased health and psychological well-being. For example, Park et al. (2010) examined the physiological effects of time in a forest atmosphere versus experiencing a cityscape and found that forest environments promote lower concentrations of cortisol, lower pulse rate, lower blood pressure, greater parasympathetic nerve activity, and lower sympathetic nerve activity than do city environments.

In addition, White and Pahl et al. (2013) showed that exposure to natural environments can help restore depleted emotional and cognitive resources and that visits to the coast, woodlands and uplands had the highest restoration value. Green space also increases creativity. Atchley, Strayer and Atchley (2012) found that exposure to nature can restore prefrontal cortex-mediated executive processes and replenish some, lower-level modules of the executive attentional system. Their research showed that immersion in nature increases performance on a creativity, problem-solving task by a full 50% and demonstrated that there is a cognitive advantage when we spend time immersed in a natural green space setting.

Green space also increases compassion and altruism. Guéguen and Stefan (2016) explored helping behavior before and after being immersed in a parkland environment and found significantly increased altruistic behavior and desire to help from green space immersion. Green space heals. Ulrich (1984) examined the impacts on hospital recovery and found that those who were exposed to windows looking out on a natural scene had significantly shorter postoperative stays. And our connection with nature also increases our levels of mindfulness and sense of inner well-being (Howell et al., 2011), showing that green space can connect us back with our deeper more balanced selves.

So being out in nature, in a green environment, is good for us. No real surprise there. Unfortunately in our busy lives, we don't always have as much time and opportunity as needed to get out into the bushland, forests and nature. The good news is that we may not need to. In a study to compare the restorative effects of the natural environment with that of an indoor simulation of green space, Kjellgren and Buhrkall (2010), found that while real nature worked best, nevertheless, even a simulation of being in green space facilitated stress reduction and enhanced restoration.

Research by Korpela et al. (2010) also found that the more stressed a person is and the more worries they have about money and work, the less often they engage in restorative green space experiences. Yet, when they do engage with such environments the more restorative the experiences are. So whilst in our busy, stressed lives we may not have the time or inclination to jump in the car and head out to a forest or green space, however we can easily take a quick guided visualization Journey to a restorative virtual green space in our mind. And the research on visualization and guided imagery we described in the previous section tells us that an imagined experience is almost as impactful and beneficial as the real thing!

Blue Mind

'Blue Mind' is the term for the neurological, psychological and emotional changes our brains experience when we are close to or experiencing water, such as the ocean, rivers and lakes. In his seminal book on the subject, Nichols (2015), describes *"The surprising science that shows how being near, in, on, or under water can make you happier, healthier, more connected, and better at what you do."* The research shows there are deep and positive impacts to our brains and bodies when we are close to water.

"It's clear that water can help us access the state called 'flow', where we connect to the default mode network, or daydreaming parts of our brain. This can restore our ability to focus and perform cognitive and creative tasks with greater ease."

W.J. Nichols

Völker and Kistemann (2011) in a systematic review of research on blue mind found that clear benefits for health and well-being related to being around water could be identified. Additionally, direct health benefits have been found in both numerous experimental studies and cross-sectional surveys. For example, White et al. (2016) showed that individuals living near the coast are generally healthier and happier than those living inland. And research by Wheeler et al. (2012) showed that the coastal environment provides significant benefits in terms of stress reduction and leaves people feeling calmer, more relaxed and more revitalized than visits to city parks or the countryside. So blue mind is even stronger that green space in terms of reducing stress and bringing autonomic balance.

And our love affair with blue mind starts young. That we find glossy and glistening surfaces, such as those of water, attractive and engaging, (even at a gut level), is shown by research with infants and toddlers. Coss, Ruff and Simms (2003) for example, showed that children will mouth bright glossy reflective surfaces significantly more often than dull surfaces and evidence drinking-like behaviors with those surfaces. Yes it's true. We like the sensory experiences of water.

Even blue light by itself is beneficial. Iyilikci, Aydin and Canbeyli (2009) showed that blue but not red light stimulation in the dark has antidepressant effects in alleviating behavioral despair. Blue light is calming. So blue space and mind are salutary for our heart, mind and souls. As Völker and Kistemann (2013), in their paper entitled, *"I'm always entirely happy when I'm here!"*, coastal environments and blue mind experiences enhance human health and well-being.

> *"Blue space may be interpreted as a therapeutic landscape and restorative and salutogenic experience."*

> Völker & Kistemann, 2013

Being around water, whether it's the ocean, rivers, ponds, lakes or streams is healthy, calming and restorative. Its impacts are stronger than those of green space. The benefits accrue to both mind and body (White et al., 2013). And add in the power of visualization and guided imagery to this and we have a potent recipe for bringing balance and regeneration during guided Journeys by combining both green space and blue mind.

Symbolism and Metaphor

> *"Symbolism is an instrument of knowledge and the most ancient and fundamental method of expression, one which reveals aspects of reality which escape other modes of expression."*

> J.C. Cooper

We live in a world of symbols and meaning. As the great psychoanalyst, Carl Jung, pointed out in his seminal work on *'Man and His Symbols'*, we are embedded in a world of symbolism and they form a key part of how we make deep meaning and how our unconscious mind works.

"The collective unconscious consists of the sum of the instincts and their correlates, the archetypes. Just as everybody possesses instincts, so he also possesses a stock of archetypal images."

Carl Jung

"Throughout the ages, stories with certain basic themes have recurred over and over, in widely disparate cultures; emerging like the goddess Venus from the sea of our unconscious."

Joan D. Vinge

The unconscious mind speaks in symbol, myth and metaphor. These symbols, as work in the field of Symbolic Anthropology has shown, span across cultures and time. So from this deep reservoir of unconscious archetypes, we are quite often swayed, without realizing it, by the power of these symbols and their attendant associations.

Beginning in the 1930s, Carl Jung's students started collecting mythological, ritualistic, and symbolic imagery under the auspices of The Archive for Research in Archetypal Symbolism (ARAS). The ARAS database has now grown to contain more than 17,000 images and 90,000 pages of cultural and psychological scholarly commentary on symbolic archetypes. Along with other scholars and studies in symbolic anthropology (E.g. see: Protas et al., 2001; Cooper, 1978), what has been found for example, is that birds can symbolize peace and a sense of spiritual guidance. Butterflies, often used in both myth and art symbolize and signify transformation and personal evolution. Water often represents birth, change, fertility and cleansing. In creation stories, life emerges from the primordial waters. Rain can signify cleansing and purification. Bright light is a symbol for purity, goodness, clarity and enlightenment. Rainbows represent new beginnings, hope and the fulfillment of dreams. Circles symbolize wholeness. Forests are symbols for going deep into the wisdom and mysteries of the unconscious, and individual trees often symbolize creation and life. The moon is used in many cultures to represent the rhythm of time and eternity.

These recurring themes and symbols speak to our heart, gut and mind. They influence us deeply, often outside of our conscious awareness. For this reason the following symbols and colors, (yes there is evidence for the symbolic effects of color on our autonomic and unconscious systems), are used repeatedly throughout the Journeys in this book. You may find it interesting to examine what each symbol represents and especially from an *m*BIT perspective.

Trees

Trees in mythology are often ascribed mystical powers and are connected with a sense of the spiritual. Trees also symbolize growth, nourishment and the dynamics of life. Trees can also represent knowledge and a connection to wisdom, as rooted in the earth they are reaching towards the heavens, evocative of time and eternity.

From an *m*BIT point of view, trees symbolize the gut and pelvic intelligences, their highest expressions and prime functions.

Mountains

The mountain represents transcendence, spiritual elevation and divine inspiration. It is a universal symbol of the nearness of God as it extends toward the heavens. It also symbolizes constancy, eternity, permanence, firmness, motionlessness and stillness. Mountain peaks spiritually signify the state of full or absolute consciousness and the renunciation of worldly desires.

From an *m*BIT perspective, mountains symbolize the highest expression and prime functions of the ANS and of integration and transcendence of heart and gut based needs and desires.

Rocks

Rocks are symbolic for permanence, stability and reliability. They also symbolize strength, power, refuge, protection and steadfastness. Water gushing or flowing from a rock signifies the source of living waters and the pure flow of the energy of life.

In *m*BIT terms, rocks represent the highest expression and prime functions of the gut brain – courage, strength, protection, stability.

Water

In the Taoist tradition, water is considered to be a deep aspect of wisdom. The concept here is that water takes on any form in which it is held and moves easily in the path of least resistance. The ancient Greeks believed that water, with its ability to flow from liquid to solid to vapor, was the archetypal symbol for metamorphosis and change. Native Americans considered water to be a symbol of life. And ancient Egyptians used water as the symbol for the birth of life and existence. Also as Jung pointed out, water is the commonest symbol for the unconscious mind.

From this we can see, from an *m*BIT perspective, water represents a symbol of wisdom, flow and connection/integration across and between the brains and their intuitive embodied unconscious intelligence.

Rivers

River symbolism has played an important part in many story genres. This symbolism corresponds to the creative power of nature and time. It signifies fertility as well as the moving, flowing passage of eternity.

Through the lens of *m*BIT, rivers connect with creativity and co-creativity and the integration of the prime functions of head and pelvic/reproductive intelligence centers.

Lakes and Ponds

Lakes have a strong association with symbolic aspects of the feminine archetype. Cooper (1978) notes that they are often the dwelling place of magical feminine powers, such as *"The Lady of the Lake."* In Chinese mythology, the lake symbolizes collected waters, receptive wisdom, absorption and stillness.

With *m*BIT, lakes and ponds can represent pelvic or reproductive intelligence and autonomic coherence and integration.

Mirrors

Mirrors symbolize truth, self-realization, wisdom, mind and the deeper connection to the soul. They are also used to represent the *'mirror of the universe'*; the reflection of divine intelligence and the clear shining surface of supreme truth shining in their reflection. The clear reflection in the mirror, such as the surface of a pond or a pool, is also used to signify man's knowledge of himself.

Looked at through *m*BIT eyes, mirrors represent the deeper connection of the head to the heart (via mirror neurons and the vagal eyes-face-heart circuit) and the emergence of inner wisdom to the surface of consciousness.

Birds

As Roque (2010) points out, birds are spiritual messengers and have a symbolic creative role in bringing forth wisdom in a person's life. Across cultures and time, birds such as the owl have represented intuition and wisdom, the hawk as vision and perspective, or a spiritual messenger, the hummingbird symbolizes enjoyment of life and the crow, of mystery and magic.

From an *m*BIT perspective, birds symbolize the integration of body and mind and all of the multiple brains to evoke the emergence of wisdom.

Butterflies

Butterflies are deep and powerful representations of life and re-birth (Haynes, 2013). Many cultures associate the butterfly with our souls and as symbols of resurrection. Around the world and across cultures, people view the butterfly as representing endurance, change, hope, and life.

In terms of *m*BIT, butterflies symbolize emergence of creativity and co-creativity and integration between gut, heart, head and pelvic prime functions.

Rainbows

Lee et al. (2001) suggest that in myth and art, rainbows are seen as bridges to spiritual wisdom, linking gods with humanity. They are also seen as messengers of spiritual import. They can mean hope, harmony, connection and transformation. The rainbow holds a ubiquitous meaning of unity in numerous cultures and brings a sense of unification and connection between sky and earth.

*m*BIT would say that the rainbow therefore symbolizes the coherent connection of the multiple brains and the evoking of the emergence of higher wisdom.

Fish

Fish symbolize fecundity, procreation, life renewed and sustained – the ongoing preservation of life. In Buddhist terms, fish represent freedom from restraint and the emancipation from desires and attachments. In the ancient Celtic culture, salmon and trout were associated with sacred wells as symbols of the foreknowledge of the gods. The Chinese culture on the other hand sees fish as symbols of abundance, wealth, regeneration and harmony. In many cultures, starfish represent healing and regeneration.

In terms of *m*BIT, we can see that fish represent pelvic and gut brains and their highest expressions and prime functions.

Heart

As Cooper (1978) explicates: *"Heart is the centre of being, both physical and spiritual; the divine presence at the centre. The heart represents the 'central' wisdom of feeling as opposed to the head-wisdom of reason; both are intelligence, but the heart is also compassion."*

From an *m*BIT perspective, the ancient symbolism of heart matches precisely what the neuroscience and behavioral modeling action research of *m*BIT uncovered. It truly is the case that the symbolic insights from ancient wisdom accurately represent the nature of our heart-based intuitive and embodied intelligence.

Color Symbolism

While there is great diversity in the use and meaning of colors between cultures and even within the same culture in different time periods, nevertheless certain color meanings remain relatively constant between and across cultures and times (e.g. see Madden, Hewett & Roth, 2000; Ohtsuki, 2000; Adams & Osgood, 1973). These key color associations that have endured through time and space are also backed up by recent research on the neuroscience of color. Where there is conformance between anthropological color symbolism and scientific research, I have utilized those colors and their symbolic meanings within the Journeys.

Blue – Blue light influences the Autonomic Nervous System and decreases stress (Litscher et al., 2013; Ross, Guthrie & Dumont, 2013; Krakov, 1942). Across cultures it is considered to be calming and relaxing. Blue is the color of both the ocean and the sky and typically symbolizes serenity, stability, reliability, trust, comfort, security and inspiration (Bourn, 2011). Research shows that the color blue enhances creativity and can do so outside of conscious awareness (Mehta & Zhu, 2009). Blue is also profoundly involved in the psychological and cultural aspects of religious experience and a deep connection with the sacred (Fallon, 2014). For example, in Judaism, blue is the color for holiness and divinity; and in Hinduism it symbolizes immortality and is the color of Krishna, the god of love and divinity (Roberts, 2017).

Yellow – Bright yellow is a stimulating color and is typically associated with positive emotions, optimism, energy, excitement, sunshine, happiness and joy (Elliot, 2015; Aslam, 2006; Kaya & Epps, 2004). In the Chinese culture it symbolizes prosperity (Olesen, 2018). From an *m*BIT perspective, yellow links to heart based competencies and prime functions and is also stimulating to the sympathetic arm of the ANS.

Green – The color green is one of the most positive and relaxing colors (Kaya & Epps, 2004). It is used to symbolize nature, peace, growth, balance, vitality, revival and healing (De Bortoli & Maroto, 2001; Cooper, 1978; Jung & Franz, 1968). Studies have shown that green decreases stress and anxiety (Kutchma, 2003; Jacobs & Suess, 1975), and that green light induces the most rapid sleep onset (Pilorz, 2016). Thus we can see that from an *m*BIT point of view, green is connected with gut based prime functions with it's deep connections to immune function and self-preservation.

Voice Prosody, Tonality and the Vagus - How you speak matters

According to Polyvagal theory (Porges, 2011), a theory about the evolution and neurophsyiological impacts of the Autonomic Nervous System (ANS), both the ears and the voice (larynx and pharynx) are innervated by the ANS, and in particular a key part of the ANS, the vagus nerve, is influenced deeply by differing sounds, tones and frequencies. For example low rumbling tones can signify danger and stimulate the Sympathetic arm of the Autonomic Nervous System. On the other hand, when people are depressed, their voice prosody and tonal range changes, they speak with flat tonal affect, and this is measurable and detectable by computer systems so that software can predict when someone is in an active phase of depression versus when they are no longer depressed (Yang, Fairbairn & Cohn, 2013).

You can experience this for yourself by talking in a slow, flat, low tone and note how it shifts your emotional experience. Most people feel it in their heart, which is not surprising as one arm of the vagus nerve is called by Dr. Stephen Porges (developer of Polyvagal theory), the *voice-face-heart circuit*.

Of course, ancient wisdom traditions have known about the power of sound for thousands of years. Most use the chanting of prayers and mantras ('*mantra*' is a Sanskrit word for "sound tool") to help guide neurophysiological states. For example, the Dalai Lama says that for clarity of mind and in these acceleratingly stressful times, it is beneficial to chant or listen to a mantra such as '*Om*'. Each mantra has its own tonal effects on the nervous system. And there is growing research to back this up.

For example there are studies showing that chanting Om versus other sounds (such as 'sssss' or the word 'one') has a strong impact on the Autonomic Nervous System and the emotional limbic structures of the brain, and can help calm people down (Kalyani et al., 2011; Bernardi et al., 2001; Telles, Nagarathna & Nagendra, 1995). Other studies have shown that chanting Om and other mantras can increase memory (Naidu et al., 2014) and mental alertness and attention (Pradhan & Godse Derle, 2012; Telles, Nagarathna & Nagendra, 1998). And you don't have to do the chanting, even simply listening to a mantra has been shown to increase reaction speed and concentration ability (Malhotra et al., 2014).

The tonal experience of listening to music also influences the ANS greatly, calming it down. For example, relaxing *new age* music has been found to strongly shift heart rate variability and calm the Autonomic System (Pérez-Lloret et al., 2014). And both listening to relaxing music and mantra chanting decrease pain and improve mood and sleep quality, with the mantra having a slightly stronger effect compared to simply listening to the music (Innes et al., 2018).

So tonal prosody makes a difference and pairing this with relaxing background music can induce positive state shifts with lasting effects on many cognitive, emotional and bodily functions. This means that when you take someone on a Journey, make sure you speak slowly, calmly and evenly, using voice prosody and tonality that is both uplifting and calming. It's a lot like how you would speak to a child, and every parent knows that the tone you use when speaking with a child can either calm them or irritate them. And for guided Journeys we definitely want to influence the vagus nerve to bring our Journeyers into a calm Autonomically balanced and receptive state.

And if you have learned the Milton Model of NLP, please don't use the "*Milton voice*" and speak like Milton... For as Milton himself pointed out in a video recording talking about creating a favorable climate for hypnosis to work (Erickson, 1979): "*And don't try to imitate my voice or my cadence. Just discover your own, be your own natural self. I've seen dozens of scores of men try and imitate me. It's a hollow pretense... If you talk very rapidly do so. If you talk very softly do so. If you talk slowly, do so. But be yourself.*"

Milton spoke like he did, in a very low, slow tone with flat affect and prosody because his vocal cords had been damaged as a young child by polio. His voice was paralyzed and he had to re-learn how to speak. His voice tone actually creates a dorsal vagal '*depressed*' state. And that's not truly what we want for our Journeys. We certainly want calm, relaxing; but also energizing and delighting in our Journeyers experience. So as Milton encourages, "*be your own natural self,*" and speak in a mellifluous and melodious manner, with your own beautiful vocal range. Use lots of pauses and speak in a cadence that matches the breathing rate you want your Journeyer to entrain to. Use your voice like a natural musical instrument to evoke the emotions of the passages you are reading.

Bringing it all Together

So bringing all of the above together to create Guided Journeys for the heart, mind and soul, we begin each Journey by following the *m*BIT Foundational Sequence: **ANS balance >> Heart >> Head >> Heart >> Gut >> Heart** (see Appendix for more details). We also layer in the *m*BIT Highest Expressions of **Calmness/Coherence** (through balanced breathing), **Compassion, Creativity, Courage**

and Co-creativity. We utilize entrancing and artfully guiding NLP Milton Patterns and Ainslie Meares Mental Ataraxis meditation techniques. And we make extensive use of deep archetypal symbolism. At a subtle level, the Journeys use specific wordings to evoke combinations of tones and ventral vagal sounds to calm and energize the ANS and evoke heart and gut prime functions. We also utilize the power of creative visualization allied with green space and blue mind to evoke deeply regenerative states. In addition, the Journeys use suggestion and embedded commands to influence the unconscious mind and evoke the emergence of deeper intuitive wisdom. Ultimately, each Journey is inspired by *m*BIT and NLP to uplift the heart, delight the mind and deeply relax the soul.

Finally, each of the Journeys has a symbolic generative gift and theme. These are:

1. **High on an Alpine Path** – provides an *important message* of wisdom and vitality.

2. **Deep into the Heart of the Forest** – offers a *gift of wisdom* from the earth.

3. **Floating on an Ocean Wave** – delivers a *generative treasure* from the ocean.

4. **Safe in a peace-filled Log Cabin** – evokes a mindful *dream about deep purpose.*

Exploring the Journeys

While you can certainly read this book from cover to cover to enjoy the guided visualizations for yourself, it was originally intended to be a set of scripts that you read to another person to guide them into deeply generative trance states — scripts that you can dip into and explore, one delightful experience at a time. So it's designed to allow you to look through the *Journey* content list and find what currently resonates for you and the person you are taking on the guided journey and then use that.

Each Journey should take approximately 40 to 45 minutes to complete. There are two possible endings. The first is for sleeping, allowing the Journeyer to just drift off into a beautiful night's sleep. The other ending is used to bring the Journeyer back from the experience, back to the here and now. Of course, approach and enjoy each Journey in whatever way works best for you and your Journeyer and do feel free to extemporize, enhance and creatively modify them with your own unique wisdoming. And I hope this book adds much value to your life and that by conveying new perceptions to both your and your Journeyer's mind, heart and soul that the Journeys truly bring your human spirit alive.

Hearing an Example Journey

If you'd like to enjoy being taken on one of the Journeys and having the opportunity to listen to how I use pausing, phrasing and vocal prosody to guide a Journey, please go to:

http://mbraining.bandcamp.com

where you can purchase at very, very low cost an mp3 of the first Journey – '*High on an Alpine Path*'. And I truly hope you enjoy it.

Instructions
for the
Journeys

Instructions for the Guide

As a Guide, reading the scripts will not just influence and calm your Journeyer, but the same processes will be at work in your unconscious mind and your multiple brains – so you also gain the benefits as you read and guide your Journeyer through these generative experiences. As you guide the Journey, you need to ensure you put yourself into and then maintain the state of Highest Expression of your multiple brains (Autonomic Balance, Compassion in your Heart, Creativity in your Head, Courage in your Gut, Co-creativity in your Pelvic Intelligence) to entrain both yourself and your Journeyer.

You also need to focus on utilizing the most optimal voice tonality and prosody, and ensure you are evoking the ventral vagal (voice-face-heart) circuit. A key way to do this is to ensure you keep in balanced breathing yourself and to hold a wonderful smile on your face and in your heart. If you are en-joy-ing yourself then it will come across in your non-verbals.

In terms of pausing and timing, you will want to pace this for balanced breathing of both yourself and your Journeyer. So don't rush. Pause. Breathe. Enjoy.

Steps to follow as you guide the Journey

1. In conjunction with your Journeyer, pick a Journey, allowing both your and their wisdom and intuition – your aligned hearts, heads and guts – to be your guide as to which Journey to choose this time around.

2. Read through the Journey script at least once silently to familiarize yourself with it and to get a sense of the pausing

and pacing. Then read the script out loud to practice your tonality, prosody and voicing. Make the script your *'own'* so that you can read it with your own authentic style.

3. Allow approximately 45 minutes for the whole Journey process.

4. Find a private, safe, comfortable place to sit or lay back.

5. Remove any distractions and potential interruptions such as the phone, loud noise, over-bright light etc. Adjust clothing, eyeglasses and footwear.

6. You may (depending on your own and your Journeyer's preference) wish to play some calming meditative music gently in the background. Research has shown that relaxing music influences mood and autonomic state (Thoma et al., 2013) and that positive mood induction effects of music increases positive self-evaluation (Brown & Mankowski, 1993). So if it's appropriate, find some deeply calming music, such as meditative 528Hz music that you can search for on youtube, and play it quietly in the background to help evoke a restful mood state. Both you and your Journeyer will benefit from it.

7. Set the context and *'scene'* for your Journeyer. Tell your Journeyer before you start, *"In this deep and intuitive Journey that I'll be guiding you on, I'm going to invite you to see, feel and experience things in your imagination. Whatever way works best for you. You may actually see things in your mind's eye, or not. You may hear, feel, smell and taste things in a virtual way, or not. Whatever happens in your inner sensory landscape as the Journey*

unfolds is beautifully ok. Some people just drift off and allow the words to flow over them. Others follow the words and process deeply and easily. Just allow the Journey to unfold in the most natural way for you, delighting in the experience and relaxation. And while doing the Journey with your eyes closed is often an optimal way to truly get into the guided visualization, you can open your eyes at any time if you need to come back into the room. Or you can keep them closed until the end. Just relax into this and allow yourself the space to deeply let go and enjoy this guided creative Journey."

8. Begin to read the Journey script to your Journeyer. Read slowly, allowing the Journeyer pauses and time to follow the guided visualization processes. Read with a poetic rhythm. Make your voice an instrument of flow. And use a resonant and mellifluous voicing. Your voice prosody influences their autonomic nervous system. So use your voice to relax, to go deeeeeep, to evoke emotion, to calm, to enliven. Use your voice, pausing and breathing as a beautiful instrument to evoke a wondrous Journey experience.

9. Use your sensory acuity to calibrate your Journeyer, to notice what is happening for them. Make sure you look at them and not just at the words in the book. Pace their breathing to match your words. If the next sentence says, "*as you breathe in*", watch for the rise and fall of their chest to pace them so that your words are said as they begin the next in-breath.

10. Have a box of tissues handy. As people relax deeply, their eyes or noses can begin to run, this is a natural parasympathetic response. Also, sometimes when people

have been very stressed, and they finally let go and come back to a more parasympathetic state, emotions that were held in check may come up, and so they may find themselves gently crying. This is a healing parasympathetic response and you can support them by just being there, holding wise balanced space (remember to keep breathing in a balanced way yourself) and telling them something like, *"that's right, you can allow these natural emotions and processes to just flow, to work themselves through, everything is ok, it is all ok, you are ok, just allow those emotions to surface and then dissipate, thoughts and emotions arise and pass away, you are safe, you are relaxed, I am here with you and for you, and you can just breathe now, evenly and easily and come back to a place of balance and calm and joy when you are ready."* And allow the person the time to just come back into a more balanced way of being, and when they are ready continue the Journey, or if they prefer, to stop the Journey, have a glass of cleansing water and perhaps go for a gentle walk.

11. When the Journey is complete, bring both yourself and your Journeyer gently and fully back to conscious awareness. Give the Journeyer a few minutes to sit or lay in silence, absorbing the feelings, intuitions and insights and any learnings from the Journey.

Key processes to focus on as a Guide

Safety and Protection – Make sure your Journeyer feels safe and protected. This is a key prime function of the gut brain and if it feels or intuits that the person isn't safe it will block the Journey from truly unfolding for them. So resonate a sense of calm safety, speak in a voice that expresses protection, care and safety, and truly hold a sense of being the Guide as protector and nurturer.

Permission and Acceptance – People, at the heart level, need to feel they have permission to do the Journey in their own way, that whatever they are doing is right and ok. That there's no *"right"* way that they have to follow. So ensure they feel your deep acceptance and that there is no failure, only a wonderful emergent and unfolding process that is creatively just right for them and where they are in their life right now.

Connection – We all need to feel a sense of connection, both between each other and within ourselves. This connection starts at the heart, with compassion, and spreads to head and gut. One of the easiest ways to evoke connection is to breathe compassion and appreciation into your heart and then spread that up into your head, down into your gut and out into the field around you. The heart's electromagnetic field has been scientifically shown to spread many meters around each person and to entrain the heart rate of others in that field. So, as you start the Journey and throughout the process, keep radiating a sense of love, connection, acceptance and safety. The Journeyer's multiple brains will sense your messages and entrain their mind and body into an optimal state to truly, really and deeply enjoy the Journey you are guiding them on.

Instructions for the Journeyer

"The clearer and stronger your intention, the more quickly and easily your creative visualization will work."

Shakti Gawain

As a Journeyer, listening to the guided visualization scripts read to you by your Guide, you will easily find that they influence and calm your mind, body and your multiple brains and provide a deeply generative experience. One of the most enjoyable and peaceful ways to listen to a Guided Journey is to simply relax, breathe evenly and easily, with approximately 6-seconds in-breath and 6-seconds out-breath, and just drift off.

Don't try to specifically focus on the words, just simply allow your attention to be diffuse, relaxed and calm. The idea is to let the words flow over and into your unconscious mind and allow whatever imagery or sensory experience the words evoke to come into your mind.

1. Find yourself a calm and peaceful place, lay down or sit back and relax.

2. In conjunction with your Guide, select the Journey whose theme resonates with you and that your intuition thinks, feels and perceives is right for you now.

3. As your Guide begins to read the Journey out loud to you, give yourself the gift of a lovely calming time of regeneration and rejuvenation. Your mind and body relaxing. Your head, heart and gut deeply absorbing, accepting, appreciating and digesting the positive messages of love, kindness, creativity, courage, co-creativity and wisdoming. You deserve to enjoy this deeply generative experience. And you can allow the *m*BIT Journey for your heart, mind and soul to help you in minding more wisdom in your life.

4. As the intuitive Journey unfolds allow yourself to see, feel and experience things in your imagination in whatever way works best for you. You may actually see things in your mind's eye, or not. You may hear, feel, smell and taste things in a virtual way, or not. Whatever happens in your inner sensory landscape as the Journey unfolds is beautifully ok.

5. Some people just drift off and allow the words to flow over them. Others follow the words and process deeply and easily. Just allow the Journey to unfold in the most natural way for you, delighting in the experience and relaxation. And while doing the Journey with your eyes closed is often an optimal way to truly get into the guided visualization, you can open your eyes at any time if you need to come back into the room. Or you can keep them closed until the end.

6. Just relax into this and allow yourself the space to deeply let go and enjoy your guided creative Journey.

"Every moment of your life is infinitely creative and the universe is endlessly bountiful..."

Shakti Gawain

Instructions for Personal Use - The Guide as the Journeyer

Taking into account all of the instructions above for both Guide and Journeyer... When you'd like to take a Journey yourself and will be your own Guide:

1. Pick a Journey, allow your intuition and your aligned heart, head and gut, be your guide to which Journey to choose.

2. Find a private, safe, comfortable place to sit or lay back.

3. Remove any distractions and potential interruptions such as the phone, loud noise, over-bright light etc.

4. Begin to read the Journey script to yourself, allowing yourself pauses and time to follow the guided visualization processes. You may also prefer to read the script out loud and record it using your phone or other recording device and then play this back to yourself via earbuds or headphones. That way you can more deeply sink into the experience.

5. When the Journey is complete, bring yourself gently and fully back to conscious awareness. Give yourself a few minutes to sit or lay in silence, absorbing the feelings, intuitions and insights and any learnings from the Journey.

Journey 1

HIGH ON AN ALPINE PATH...

[Read the following guided visualization script with a slow, gentle and mellifluous voice, allowing time for pauses and space for your Journeyer to breathe slowly and evenly in time with your voice and to go deep into the creativity of their own experience of your words.]

Begin now by finding a place to safely and gently relax...

Start by taking a deep easy breath and quietly, calmly and slowly begin to center your mind and center your self... Take a deep, deep breath and slowly exhale any tension from your body and your mind...

Here, now, as you listen easily to the sound of my voice, allow yourself to calmly begin to drift off... And as you do, begin also to gently and easily breathe in and breathe out, in a balanced, even, easy way... So that your in-breath and out-breath are of the same equal duration. Breathing approximately 6-seconds in, and 6-seconds out.

And as you continue to breathe, easily and evenly, calmly and gently, allow your beautiful attention to come slowly into the region

of your heart, so that with every breath, you are deeply and effortlessly breathing a sense of peace and calm and ease into the region of your beautiful heart.

And as you continue to breathe, calmly and effortlessly, easily and evenly, allow this beautiful, gentle sense of ease, peace and wellness to begin to expand from your heart up into your head... With each in-breath up from your heart to your head, and slowly, slowly, gently, easily on each out-breath down deep into your beautiful gut. Your mind calming, your belly softening. Breathing in ease and calming peace, breathing out any tension from your body... Breathing in peace, breathing out tension. Breathing peace into your heart, breathing wonderful calm deep down into your gut.

And here, now, as you continue to breathe so easily and peacefully, begin also to gently relax your muscles in your body starting from your feet and moving upwards. You can easily allow the muscles of your feet to become relaxed, relaxing so easily, and with each balanced breath that you are taking, you might allow yourself to feel your feet becoming even more loose, comfortable and more deeply relaxing. Breathing in soooo deeply, breathing out soooo easily... It is natural to relax, all natural, to let yourself relax, your body relaxing, your mind calming and at ease...

And allow yourself to let this beautiful sense of relaxation begin to spread to your calves... you might notice your calves are becoming warm, heavy and relaxed, the muscles smoothing out, softening, relaxing easily and completely letting go. You can feel this easily and deeply. A deep sense of relaxing peace moving from your feet to your calves. And this delicious warmth can begin spreading from your calves to your thighs, gently allowing your relaxing attention to concentrate so easily and effortlessly into this beautiful spreading, warm feeling in your legs, as you soooo easily continue to breathe in airs of relaxation... and breathing, now, gently, out airs of any residual tensing... inhaling calm, exhaling peace, easily and effortlessly...

Noticing how your legs are wonderfully relaxing now, here, warm and heavy, as you hear the sound of my voice, as it washes over and through you and allows your conscious mind to calmly and gently concentrate or not, on the good feelings of deeply relaxing in your legs, your legs feeling so very loose and so relaxed, heavy and supported, calmly being, deeply relaxing, as you so very deeply and truly enjoy the calm feelings of relaxation in your legs for a moment or two...

And now, in your own time, relaxing here, begin to allow your wonderful sense of relaxation to spread from your legs into your buttocks and pelvic area... you might begin to feel your hips settle, the muscles softening and relaxing. As you get a deep, deep sense of inner peace, that allows you to begin relaxing even more deeply now, and as you do, just notice how your sense of peace and relaxation spreads deeper and deeper into your gut and abdomen... Relaxing every organ in your gut. Letting your sense of peace flow deeply within. Easily relaxing your gut and abdomen, and now relaxing your back, every muscle in your back gently becoming so very relaxed, at ease, loose and wonderfully comfortable now.

And you might allow this deep sense of relaxation to spread along your spine and up into your chest, into your shoulders, feeling the warmth and heaviness as your body settles into whatever surface supports you now. And as you do, allow your wonderful calming sense of relaxation to travel into your hands, your relaxing arms and hands, allowing them to become even more relaxed and limp, without tension, free, natural, easy, calm…

With your arms heavy at your side, warm, loose and relaxing… gently open your mouth slightly, your lips gently part and let the muscles of your mouth relax. Your tongue soft, your jaw loose, relaxing your entire face, easily, calmly, lovingly. Your eyes gently relaxed and floating in their sockets, so deeply relaxing, your eyelids heavy and relaxing, any residual tension draining out of your face. Your face smoothing out, relaxing, softening, calming. Your temples and forehead so smooth, calm and so relaxed…

Your face is smooth, unwrinkled, calm. A deep sense of peace and calm, that with every breath, you feel flowing from your heart and gut up to your face and deeply into your wonderful head. Allowing your mind to relax, letting it be free, floating. Your body sinking heavily, easily into the relaxing surface that is supporting you now, so relaxed, your mind free, at ease and floating gently in this deep sense of relaxing peaceful now…

You are deeply, deeply relaxed, truly really calm. Your mind is smooth, unwrinkled, calm. Your body is at ease. You are safe. You are at peace in your heart, at peace deep within your mind, at peace deep, deep within your body… The relaxation is all through you, and so is the calm that goes with it, the calm of it is part of you, it is all through your heart, gut and body and all through your mind. Your calm pervades you, you let yourself go with it, you let yourself go more and more completely, with each breath you let yourself go, and as you do, you let go of your breath, allowing it to be automatic and easy, you are deeply relaxing, calming, floating, nothing matters, nothing else matters. Just you at ease and at peace...

And as this wonderful sense of ease and inner peace flows through and within you, with every even, easy breath... now, here, let us begin once more to go even deeper and deeper into a joy filled and delightful inner journey... an alpine journey... a journey of easily guided visualization, where you can follow along or not, as most deeply suits you, and allow the imagery and deep sensory experience to unfold with delight, or as you prefer, in whatever way works for you, to allow my voice, here, now, to flow around you as you consciously drift off, beautifully and easily...

And now... I want you to begin to simply and easily imagine yourself sitting in a field of grass. Picture yourself sitting... in a field of grass, a field of alpine grass. Just see yourself sitting comfortably, relaxed. Around you, you might notice that the grass is low, a mixture of green and dried yellow. Here and there it is tufted, and in places there are patches of shrub, and one or two small trees. Easily and effortlessly look around you now and notice the grass, the small trees and shrubs, the colors of the grass and sky. The beauty of nature...

And you may notice, as you look... at the base of one of the trees, you can see a small, speckled bird is foraging for food. Calmly, you see the bird pecking at small seeds, and it sees you, and in its heart, knowing you are safe, it continues calmly and unworried.

It is a beautiful day, sitting relaxing and calming in the grass. The sun is shining overhead, warming. You feel the sun shining overhead, warming. You feel it deeply. Your heart is at peace and filled with joy for the beauty of the day. Your gut is deeply, calmly relaxed. You are safe, and all is well in your world. Your mind is at ease. And the sky is the deepest of blues. "Beautiful!" you think, and smile. You take a deep, deep easy breath, and gently exhale the warm smell of fresh grass, with a deep and relaxing sigh. Picture your self now taking a deep, deep breath, and gently relaxing with a deep and easy sigh. And a beautiful easy smile. Smiling from your heart. Smiling deeply from within.

And... slowly and gently, you take another deep breath and again exhale, with a beautiful, soothing sigh. Ahh! A breeze is gently blowing, you may notice that you feel it in your hair and on your face. The air is clean, cool and healing. You breathe deeply again, and sigh, relaxing into the day with your beautiful wonderful smile. The sun is warming, the breeze is gently cooling, you are just right.

And gently and easily, you begin to look up ahead, across the field, you can see a mountain, your Mountain! It is a great mountain, strong and beautiful. Rising majestically above your field of alpine grass. For the most part you can notice, it is tree covered, but high, high above you might see that the top is bare of trees. Just rocks and alpine tundra. An olive green, a relaxing green, that contrasts with the colors of the rocks and the deeper greens of the lower tree covered slopes.

Looking easily around, you begin to see in the distance, many more mountains. Dark bluey-green in color. None however, as big and beautiful as your mountain, just up ahead.

Easily, and without effort, you stand and stretch. You feel the breeze around your body, the sun on your face. You breathe deeply, smile and begin effortlessly walking across the grass to a track, tanny-brown, that you now see threading its way across the field and up the lower slopes of the mountain. You reach the track easily, and stepping onto it, begin the journey upwards.

As you walk, gliding easily along the track, you may notice that the path is a mixture of colors; reds, browns, and the blues and greys of rock and gravel. And as you gently become aware of the sound of your footfalls on the loose rocks of the path, you can notice each footstep resounding inside your head and body. You hear your footfalls resounding deeply inside your head and body. And this wonderful sound of peaceful rhythmic movement, easily fills your awareness, at first, almost as proof, that you are making your way effortlessly upwards.

And gradually and imperceptibly, your awareness of the sound of your travel disappears, to the sound of grasshoppers and cicadas echoing from the heather and grasses on the hillside surrounding you. As the crunching of your footfalls on the path diminishes, so too, does your feeling of walking, and instead, you find yourself gliding even more effortlessly up the path, as it winds its way towards the top of the mountain.

You are gliding, almost floating, upwards along the path, through heather and grass and low shrubbery. Now, all you hear is the low and relaxing drone of insects in the heather, mixed with the chirruping of grasshoppers.

You breathe deeply, smelling the honey-like fragrance of gorse and heather, as it brushes against your calves. The air tastes clean and fresh. You can taste it so easily in your lungs. Healing. Relaxing. Giving you peaceful energy. The mountain air smells and tastes divine. Filling your senses with delight. A deep sense of joy suffusing your heart and gut with every breath. And up, there, you begin to notice on the mountainside above, small pools of white wildflowers, and, on the sides of the track, mingled with heather, you can now see pink, yellow and purple colored alpine flowers.

As you continue to glide along the path, you gradually begin to notice the winds call in your ears, keeping you cool, on this beautiful, sun-filled day. You are happy to be where you are now, and, breathe deeply once again, relaxing. And looking down, you see a tan and yellow butterfly, resting on a rock, also soaking in the healing energies of the sun. Next to the butterfly, is a larger brown rock, covered in pastel green moss. You look at the rock and the butterfly, enjoying their heart-felt beauty and then continue past, easily onwards and upwards.

The path is quite narrow now, and the soft yellow-brown alpine heather, knee length, almost caressing your thighs as you pass, is like an expensive, soft carpet, spread across the hillside. Such a peaceful and beautiful sight, you think, and again breathe deeply and evenly, sigh and smile.

As you gently begin to get higher, the path winds around and up the mountain. Looking down, you see the folds of tree lined gullies and valleys below. Looking easily up, you see wispy white streaks of cloud in a perfect blue sky, azure overhead, but towards the horizon, pale, pale blue. The breeze drops for a second, and you notice the sounds of a river in the valley below being carried upwards along with the gentle scraw and cry of birds.

And almost at the same time, you see a small, speckled, brown bird, running along the path up ahead. Like you, it too, seems to glide along the path calmly and effortlessly, and almost seems to be leading you, guiding you onwards. You feel a connection with it. Knowing it will keep you company, connected to your heart, connected to a deep sense of love and compassion, for yourself and others.

And as you continue to travel easily upwards, you notice that the path is slowly steepening now, and up ahead you can see the beginning of the trees, beautiful twisted and spiralled alpine trees. Their beauty filling your mind with a wonderful sense of the creativity of nature, a creativity that you so deeply, truly and really share. A creativity that is inspired by love and compassion for the world.

And now, before entering this creative, twisting, winding path through the trees, you look up, to notice the warm sun, cool wind, and feel yourself filled with the deepest sense of happiness, joy, inner-strength, gentle motivation and a serene peacefulness and calm.

You are now under the sheltering canopy of the trees, and as you glide ever upwards, you must duck and weave through the splayed branches of these beautiful trees. You can notice their smooth, silk grey and brown bark, sometimes even green and orange in places. Their slender delicate leaves. You pause for a moment and reach up to the nearest branch. Thanking the tree, you pick a choice leaf and crushing it in your hand, lift it to your face, to smell and taste the clean, sharp fragrance of its oil. The oil is healing, and so you rub the leaf against your temples. You feel its strength flowing through you.

You are whole, healthy and strong. You are calm and clear. Once again, you thank the tree for its gift, and continue gently onwards. Up through tunnels of alpine trees, with their wavering shadows. Looking down, you see, on the ground, your shadow amongst these wavering forms, and as you look, you see your shadow overtaken by the swift form of your friend the bird who has been silently accompanying you on your journey upwards, deeper and deeper into the heart of the mountain.

And gently, you look up, and as you do, you hear the bird calling to you from the trees far ahead. A beautiful heart-filling sound, like music to your soul. And it fills your heart with love and deep compassion, both for your self and for all sentient beings.

And notice... you are getting very high now, and through the wavering trees, you can just make out, if you look carefully, in glimpses, the surrounding tree covered mountains, shimmering dark, pastel green. The path turns now and steepens again. And easily you float upwards along the path, feeling free, and happy, and whole. Without a care, filled with love for this beautiful mountain. Your mountain. Strong and serene. And this tender path, full of curious delight, mystery and gentle surprise.

In the creative twisted spiralled tree branches, through which the path winds, you see pieces of bark, mottled grey, brown, green and orange, hanging, as if draped for decoration from the branches they were caught in. You see the bark, hanging. Along the path, and amongst the roots of the trees, you find white snow-daisies and small yellow flowers. On the rocks at your feet, yellow and green mosses lay patterned, as if painted by a child. The air is clean and fresh, warm and invigorating. The sweet taste of delight, the smell of peace and gentle joy. Your heart, mind and gut savoring this beautiful day in this beautiful place...

And notice... the trees are smaller now, and more separated. The path is ever steepening, and this in no way affects the ease of your progress. You are strong and relaxed. Calm and happy. You glide gently upwards, through the thinning trees, and the top of the mountain is still lost to your view. All is as it should be.

Winding ever upwards, floating easily, and at your own pace, you come across a large, dead ancient tree. Its forks, branched like arms to the sky. Pale washed green moss covers the eastern sides. Its wood scoured and creased from time. Pale, pale washed grey. Slowly, you go over and touch it, feeling love for its hard and patient life, feeling the gentle poignancy of its death. But easily and gently you let this feeling go, as the spirit of the tree speaks wordlessly to you, telling you in your heart and gut, that all is well and as it should be in cycle and circle of life.

And so, slowly and gently stepping back, you appreciate the beauty of its weatherworn form, and feel a happiness radiate through you, like warmth spreading from your stomach outwards. Quietly, you know the truth, wisdom and balance in the ebb and flow of life and nature. Knowing that the cycle continues and that the tree before you is as natural as the seedling now growing, nurtured in the rotting roots of this long-dead tree.

With life and compassionate love flowing through you, you continue upwards, noticing the whites, yellows, purples and pinks of the small wild flowers on either side of the path. They seem to be growing in greater abundance here. Seeing this, you realize that the end of the tree-line is near, and so, rounding a corner in your path, you are not at all surprised to come across a beautiful wide-open vista.

The alpine trees no longer grow here, it is too high and open, and so once again the trees give way to shrubs and heather, grasses and wild alpine flowers. Looking up, you see, as if you could reach out and touch it, the top of the mountain. It is at the end of a steep, steep climb. Above you and to the side, the mountain is dotted with the open, white faces of snow daisies and their silver-green succulent leaves.

You feel the warmth of the sun drenched open path, the air rising, bringing the smell of life, like hot toast and tea. You breathe ever so deeply, and evenly, feeling the life flow through you, healing, giving you courage and deep, deep strength.

Plainly ahead, you see the path steepen and wind its way left then right, looking for the line of least resistance. No trees here, just many-greened shrubbery and ground cover sharing with alpine grasses. The path steps over large and broken rocks, exposed and angular. You float slowly easily up this last steep, steep section, climbing over the rocks and boulders. Easily feeling your own strength and courage, like that of the mountain. A deep strong resilience. Until finally and easily, you come to rest, on the top of the world, on the top of your mountain.

In the distance, smaller mountains, blue-green with the essence of forest haze, silhouette one another, until the difference between mountain and sky is uncertain. You are here now, at the highest point of the world. You stand strong and firm, and feel the warm wind caressing you, hearing its sound echoing in your ears. You are here, now, at the top of your mountain, by yourself, happy and safe.

To your left, three butterflies, colored blue, green and yellow, play like a spinning ball in the air. You see them twist and turn, like a creative ball of fun spinning in the air. One alights on your shoulder, and sits fanning its wings in peaceful communion. Far below a hawk soars, like your spirit, free, through the air. Its shadow caressing the valley far, far below. Your beautiful companion bird sits lovingly beside you connecting deeply to your compassionate heart.

You are free and safe on the top of your mountain. Peaceful and happy. You have easily scaled to the top of the world, and are filled with a sense of achievement at its beauty, and of self-worth from your incredible alpine journey. You feel deeply kind, compassionate and good. Filled with a creativity that is guided by your immense compassion. And deeply imbued with a sense of gentle gutsy courage that allows you to put your compassionate creativity into the world to make a difference to your life and the lives of others.

You are the wisest and highest expression of your self. You feel this deeply in every cell. You know this in every way. And you will carry this wonderful sense of compassionate, creative and courageous inner self-worth deep within you always now.

And intriguingly, now, here, you can be delighted to find that your wonderful mountain journey has a message for you. A wise message that can help you live the life you truly deserve. From deep within the earth, rising up gently through your mountain, and reverberating in your heart, gut and mind, in your bones and skin, through every cell of your body, your mountain has a message of wisdom and purpose that can emerge gently into your awareness.

This message may not come to your awareness right now, it may naturally emerge in the hours and days to come. And when it does arrive, it may appear as an image or vision, as a metaphor or a simple set of words. It may come as a hunch, intuition or felt sense, a deep inner knowing. And when it arrives you will know deeply in your heart, mind and gut that this is your gift from your connection to the earth, from the universe, from your mountain. A message to support you wisely in living the most wondrous and amazing life you can live and being the wisest and most amazing person you can be.

And so filled now, with a wonderful ease, peace and compassionate love, you lay down on a small, comfortable patch of alpine grass, that you notice just to one side, and easily closing your eyes:

1. FOR SLEEPING

You begin to drift gently and easily into a deep and relaxing sleep. An easy sleep, a good sleep. Knowing that you are safe and comfortable and that all is as it should be. Knowing also, that, when you are ready, and in your own good time, you will be able to awaken easily and return from your mountain top. Feeling refreshed, calm and full of life and energy...

That you can awaken easily and effortlessly and only when you are truly ready... and that when finally you awake, as you sleep now, know that on awakening you will be able to bring a deep and ongoing sense of peace and calmnessing, of compassion, creativity and courage, to everything that you do, so that you will, when you awaken, continue to live into the highest expressing of your self in wise and wonderful ways.

Sleep deeply and peacefully now...

2. TO END THE JOURNEY

[Allow a couple of minutes of peaceful space.]

Gently allow your whole body to begin to relax, starting from your toes and moving upwards. Picture your toes relaxing, and feel the relaxation flow like warmth from your toes through your feet. Relaxing your feet, and feeling the warmth spread from your feet to your ankles. Relaxing your ankles and legs, calves and knees, and feeling this warmth spread deeply into your calves and knees. The warmth spreads slowly upwards and inwards. You are lying relaxing on the grass, on this warm and comfortable day, safe on top of your mountain...

Relaxing so deeply and easily, joyfully and calmly... and as you relax your thighs and pelvis, hips and stomach, feel the warmth spread easily up into your body, into your torso. Feel the warmth and relaxation spread into your chest and up into your spine and back, into your shoulders and down into your arms, down into your hands...

You are lying on the relaxing grass, on the top of your mountain, so safely relaxed and calm. And as you continue to sink deeply into the grass, safe and at peace, you can lay here easily, safely. Feeling the peace of the silence, the peace of the space. Thinking nothing. Your mind so totally relaxing...

Here, now, just experiencing this moment. Knowing that you are safe and free. Happy and whole. You are a beautiful and worthwhile person. Feeling the healing sun shining warmly onto your relaxing body, the wind flowing over you, its call in your ears, touching your skin. The air fragrant with delight...

You are balanced and strong, good, wise and worthwhile. Your heart is filled with peaceful love and compassion. Your mind is creative, calm and relaxed, filled with a peaceful sense of curiosity for life. Your gut and body filled with energy, life and courage. All parts of you deeply connected. Your intuitive wisdom available deeply within to help you whenever and wherever you may need in your life.

Feel the peace of this moment, feel the sun on your body, the warmth soaking through you, on the highest point of your world.

The rest of the world far, far below... You are safe and happy, on top of your mountain. A beautiful blue sky overhead, diminishing to a pale, pale blue, where it meets the mountains in the distance. You are deeply relaxed, your mind free to soar like a bird, float like a cloud, drifting, drifting, drifting, free with the wind... at peace within and without.

Taking the time to refresh your spirit. Balance your energy. Your unconscious and conscious minds working together for your wise success. Your heart filled with love and compassion for yourself and others.

Your inner and outer attention in balance. You are wise and well. And now, when you are ready, and in your own good and perfect time, here, now, you know you can come back from this delight-filled journey, and awaken now, easily, and gently open your eyes, and return from your mountain top.

Feeling refreshed, calm and full of life and energy. In your own good time, you can awaken easily now, open your eyes slowly and gently, stretch, take a deep, deep breath and return now from the mountain, refreshed and full of boundless energy...

Knowing deeply, truly and really that you will be able to bring a deep and ongoing sense of peace and calmnessing, of compassion, creativity and courage, to everything that you do, so that you will, from now on, continue to live into the highest expressing of your self in wise and wonderful ways.

Journey 2

DEEP INTO THE HEART
OF THE FOREST...

[Read the following guided visualization script with a slow, gentle and mellifluous voice, allowing time for pauses and space for your Journeyer to breathe slowly and evenly in time with your voice and to go deep into the creativity of their own experience of your words.]

Begin now by finding a place to safely and gently relax…

Start by taking a deep easy breath and quietly, calmly and slowly begin to center your mind and center your self… Take a deep, deep breath and slowly exhale any tension from your body and your mind.

Here, now, as you listen easily to the sound of my voice, allow yourself to calmly begin to drift off. And as you do, begin also to gently and easily breathe in and breathe out, in a balanced, even, easy way… So that your in-breath and out-breath are of the same equal duration. Breathing approximately 6-seconds in, and 6-seconds out.

And as you continue to breathe, easily and evenly, calmly and gently, allow your beautiful attention to come slowly into the region

of your heart, so that with every breath, you are deeply and effortlessly breathing a sense of peace and calm and ease into the region of your beautiful heart...

And as you continue to breathe, calmly and effortlessly, easily and evenly, allow this beautiful, gentle sense of ease, peace and wellness to begin to expand from your heart up into your head. With each in-breath up from your heart to your head, and slowly, slowly, gently, easily on each out-breath down deep into your beautiful gut. Your mind calming, your belly softening... Breathing in ease and calming peace, breathing out any tension from your body. Breathing in peace, breathing out tension. Breathing peace into your heart, breathing wonderful calm deep down into your gut.

And here, now, as you continue to breathe so easily and peacefully, begin also to gently relax your muscles in your body starting from your feet and moving upwards. You can easily allow the muscles of your feet to become relaxed, relaxing so easily, and with each balanced breath that you are taking, you might allow yourself to feel your feet becoming even more loose, comfortable and more deeply relaxing. Breathing in soooo deeply, breathing out soooo easily... It is natural to relax, all natural, to let yourself relax, your body relaxing, your mind calming and at ease...

And allow yourself to let this beautiful sense of relaxation begin to spread from your feet to your calves... you might notice your calves are becoming warm, heavy and relaxed, the muscles smoothing out, softening, relaxing easily and completely letting go. You can feel this easily and deeply. A deep sense of relaxing peace moving from your feet to your calves...

And this delicious warmth can begin spreading from your calves into your thighs, gently allowing your relaxing attention to concentrate so easily and effortlessly into this beautiful spreading, warm feeling in your legs, as you sooo easily continue to breathe in airs of relaxation, and breathing, now, gently, out airs of any residual tensing, inhaling calm, exhaling peace, easily and effortlessly...

Noticing how your legs are wonderfully relaxing now, here, warm and heavy, as you hear the sound of my voice, here, as it washes over and through you and allows your conscious mind to calmly and gently concentrate or not, on the good feelings of deeply relaxing in your legs, your legs feeling so very loose and so very relaxed, heavy and supported, calmly being, deeply relaxing, as you so very deeply and truly enjoy the calm feelings of relaxation in your legs for a moment or two more...

And now, in your own time, relaxing here, begin to allow your wonderful sense of relaxation to spread from your legs into your buttocks and pelvic area... you might begin to feel your hips settle, the muscles softening and relaxing. As you get a deep, deep sense of inner peace, that allows you to begin relaxing even more deeply now, and as you do, just notice how your sense of peace and relaxation spreads deeper and deeper into your gut and abdomen.

Relaxing every organ in your gut. Letting your sense of peace flow deeply within. Easily relaxing your gut and abdomen, and now relaxing your back, every muscle in your back gently becoming so very relaxed, at ease, loose and wonderfully comfortable now...

And you might allow this deep sense of relaxation to spread along your spine and up into your chest, into your shoulders, feeling the warmth and heaviness as your body settles into whatever surface supports you now. And as you do, allow your wonderful calming sense of relaxation to travel into your hands, your relaxing arms and hands, allowing them to become even more relaxed and limp, without tension, free, natural, easy, calm…

With your arms heavy at your side, warm, loose and relaxing… gently open your mouth slightly, your lips gently parting and let the muscles of your mouth completely relax. Your tongue soft, your jaw loose, relaxing your entire face, easily, calmly, lovingly… Your eyes gently relaxed and floating in their sockets, so deeply relaxing, your eyelids heavy and relaxing, any residual tension draining out of your face. Your face smoothing out, relaxing, softening, calming. Your temples and forehead so smooth, calm and so relaxed…

Your face is smooth, unwrinkled, calm. A deep sense of peace and calm, that with every breath, you feel flowing from your heart and gut up to your face and deeply into your wonderful head. Allowing your mind to relax, letting it be free, floating. Your body sinking heavily, easily into the relaxing surface that is supporting you now, here, so relaxed, your mind free, at ease and floating gently in this deep sense of relaxing peaceful now…

You are deeply, deeply relaxed, truly really calm. Your mind is smooth, unwrinkled, calm. Your body at ease. You are safe. You are at peace in your heart, at peace deep within your mind, at peace deep, deep, deep within your body… The relaxation is all through you now, and so is the calm that goes with it, the calm of it is part of you, it is all through your heart, gut and body and all through your mind. Your calm pervades you, you let yourself go with it, you let yourself go more and more completely, with each easy breath you let yourself go, and as you do, you even let go of your breath, allowing it to be automatic and easy, you are deeply relaxing, calming, floating, nothing matters, nothing else matters. Just you at ease and at peace...

And as this wonderful sense of ease and inner peace flows through and within you, with every even easy breath... now, here, let us begin once more to go even deeper and deeper into a joy filled and delightful inner journey... a forest journey... a journey of easily guided visualization, where you can follow along or not, as most deeply suits you, and allow the imagery and deep sensory experience to unfold with delight, or as you prefer, in whatever way works for you, to allow my voice, here, now, to flow around you as you consciously drift off, beautifully and easily...

And now... I want you to begin to simply and easily imagine yourself drifting, at peace. Drifting. Around you are clouds, white, soft, fluffy clouds. You are drifting in a world of white. Safely, naturally, at ease. You hear and see nothing, the world is a warm, gentle, white, safe place. There is just you, drifting, amongst fluffy white clouds, soft and gentle. And with a serene magic the clouds begin to thin and lift. And slowly, slowly your vision clears...

And you might begin to notice that at your feet you can see grasses and small twigs, leaves and pebbles... You are outside. The sky is slowly clearing and is soon a brilliant deep blue, dotted with small, soft, fluffy clouds. The day is delightfully warm and pleasant. Just right. You are feeling relaxed and serene…

And before you stands a forest, filled with strong, tall trees. And as you look around, you can notice that a path leads from where you stand, forward into its heart. Behind you is the rest of the world. In front of you stretches this peaceful, beautiful and serene forest. The sun is beaming down, warm and luscious. A breeze gently echoes in the trees. Birds sing, calling to you…

Without hesitation you begin to move gently forward, into the peaceful forest. The path is soft with fallen leaves, branches curve above, forming a tunnel, an entrance. You are drifting along the weaving, winding path, past large rounded boulders, lichen covered, weathered and worn smooth.

The sun streams through gaps in the forest ceiling, forming golden shafts in the moist clean air. You see the patterned shadows on the floor at your feet. The straight lines of branches, mosaicked blotches of shifting, wavering leaves.

The air has a clean, green fragrance that touches your face. You feel it. You breathe of it deeply and feel its healing, calming power. You can almost taste how delicious the air is in your lungs. Deeply healing. Amongst the patterned shadows at your feet you can notice subtle shades of dried leaves and bark, twigs and grasses. A rainbow of greens and browns.

In front of you, the path is veined with gnarled and twisted roots, nature's art, worn smooth and shiny on top. In the curve where they meet the soil, are gathered washes of leaves and moss. And though the path is uneven, you find no difficulty, but drift easily along it, listening to the birdsongs, whose harmonies fill your ears and fill your mind. And you feel your heart lighten with the joy of their sound.

Drifting along, happy and serene, and filled with deep love and compassion for the beauty and gift of life, you follow now the path as it curves to one side and weaves gradually down through a small dell. Everything is moist and moss covered, green with wavering tree ferns and sword grasses, bracken and treelets. Natures creative canvas that echoes your own deep creativity. Ahead, a small rivulet of water trickles across the path, meandering amongst moss covered, rounded rocks. You hear its joy filled gurgling, lightening your heart and filling your mind and body with the energy of life.

To the right, you might now notice a large fallen tree sloping down into the stream. Carpeted with moss, its top side is bare, but streaked and runneled as if carved by a thousand small hands.

Gliding onwards, now, here, you leave the merry, gurgling, trickling sounds of the dell and follow the path onwards. Winding amongst the giant trees, the calming incessant murmur of the wind swaying their canopy far, far above, like the surge and ebb of the sea. Dull and relaxing, always there, gently calling, punctuated only by the call of birds and the echo of your gentle footfalls on the leaf strewn path.

You are going deeper and deeper into the peaceful forest. Happy and relaxed, drifting on towards its heart. A heart filled with love, compassion and appreciation for all life. Drifting, deeper, deeper still. And around you the open walls of your forest, brown and green and safe and serene...

As far as you can see, easily, ferns and trees, large and small, some thinly growing in couplets, their branches intertwined, supporting each other, others sparse and separate, happy to grow in their own unique way. The kind and creative angles of nature's vision.

And with every step, deeper and deeper, a new vision of green and brown. A new vision of life. As you find yourself, drifting into the coolness, peace and solitude of a glade that opens out under the trees. Under their sheltering canopy, the light is subtle and filtered. It is the light of the spirit. Birds call and cry from tree to tree, never seen. The space is warm and safe. The air is pure and clean. Nature's preserve.

And this wonderful place is filled with the hidden presence of life and nature. A carpet of leaves, twigs and broken branchlets crunches, crackles and resounds as you travel easily across it. In this easy filtered light, the bark of the trees has a subtle, soft and undefined appearance, allowing your imagination to create patterns of art, patterns of newness, patterns of dreams and desires yet to be fulfilled...

The air is moist and clean. You can taste it. Around you, moss covered rocks and boulders lay scattered about. Amongst them, slowly rotting logs, hollowed out like baskets lay filled with dirt and leaves and soft spongy wood. This is the cycle of nature. As things grow and then return to the earth to fertilize the next wave of life. So in your own life you flow with the impermanence of change and the opportunities of growth and personal evolution.

As you continue to move through the soft resilience of the curved, curled carpet of leaves, you notice that in places they are gathered so deeply that they reach to your knees. You wade, as if floating, through this rainbow of reds and browns, hearing the delightful rustle of your passing. Allowing you to cross easily to where the path winds its way, once again, deep into the heart of the forest. Your forest. Your beautiful compassionate and creative forest that renews your spirit as you flow and explore in this wonder-filled forest journey.

On and on, you drift. Low hanging branches brushing gently as you pass. A leaf floating quietly down, falling to its new home on the forest floor. Sword grasses wavering translucent in sunlit patches that filter from above.

You are in an easy, peaceful space, natural and calm. Your heart, mind and body filled with an empowering energy. Filled with life. The forest gives you wise power, fills you with gutsy courage to truly and deeply be you. The forest helps you connect with your deepest sense of intuitive wisdom, at one with nature, aligned with the empowering energies of the world.

And now, here, you are drifting past families of ferns, some towering high into the air. Others fine and delicate. Their trunks a hairy chocolate brown. Strong and majestic. Delicate and yet resilient. Able to rebound even when the lightening lit forest fires that naturally pass through this region every once in a lifetime or two, clear the forest of its undergrowth. Yet the courageous strong ferns rebound and regrow so quickly, showing a true resilience and making good use of the nutrients that the fire and life and ash provides.

Drifting under their perfect green, drooping fronds, splayed like hands to the sky, you marvel at their peaceful beauty. At the center, small baby fronds lay nestling, their heads curved in a spiral, waiting to unwrap and stretch forth to life. The compassion of the forest nurtures their growth...

Up ahead you can see that the path curves to meet a small burbling stream, clear and fresh. Its crystal waters flowing over rocks, rounded and all a'jumble, flowing under ferns, around trees. Laughing happily, joyously, playing in the world. Creativity at play.

In the distance you hear the stronger sound of falling water, as the path takes you deeper and deeper to its source, in the heart of the forest. Drifting along, curving left and right, floating through a sea of brown and green, you round the final bend in the path, to find a scene of such beauty, that your heart thrills at its sight.

Here deep within the forest, the sun shines in golden warmth. On one side you notice a torrent of water that crashes and splashes in crystal and white. Cascading and falling from a deep, clear pool higher in the forest to form a happy and cheerful stream. The pool is encircled with rocks and fine, delicate ferns. Its clear, refreshing waters well continuously from deep within the earth. Providing never ending sustenance to all life.

Next to the pool, a small glade of luscious green grass basks in the sunlight, and at the center of the clearing, stands an enormous tree. An ancient and venerable tree. This tree, old and wise, as old, almost as time itself, is the guardian of your forest. Though gnarled and weathered, it stands courageous, strong and full of wise life.

And as you stand here in this peaceful glade, you begin to feel a great delicious lethargy come slowly upon you. You begin to feel a soporific sense, a feeling so tired and heavy, and you sink gently and easily onto the warm, dry grass. Its earthy fragrance soothes you as you slowly close your eyes. The sound of the water, falling from the pool, surrounds you, caressing any tension from your face. You feel the compassionate, creative and courageous beauty of this place, as curled on the grass you drift effortlessly into a deep and dreamless sleep…

The large, wise, old tree stands firm, watching over you as you sleep, protecting you. You are safe here, at the heart of the forest, safe here to be you, where the power and life-force of nature is at its strongest. Allowing you to truly, really and deeply feel and be the highest expression of your self. Soaking in the sunlight, warm and at peace.

Drifting, happy and serene. Watched over and cared for, loved and protected. The leaves swaying gently in the branches high above, as small fluffy clouds drift lazily in the pure blue sky, like a chorus, calling you to play. Your body curled upon the grass, heavy and relaxed, dappled with sunlight flashes glistening from the crystal waters.

And as you so gently and easily rest, now, here, you may be wonderfully delighted to find that your wise ancient tree, with its roots deep in the earth, has a present to offer you... a gift... of intuitive wisdom. There is something for you to learn, some insight, or deep inner-knowing that can help you in your life. And even though you may not know consciously what that is right now, yet the wise tree can reach deep down within the earth, deep into the universe, deep into your unconscious mind, heart and soul, and help you emerge that present, now.

This wonderful new learning may help you overcome some blockage in life, or offer a new pathway forwards. It may help you evolve as a person. Or even be a spiritual gift with a message that you need to hear to help you heal, help you generate more vitality in your life, help you be truly, really and deeply you. It can help you become even more successful now, more connected, more compassionate, creative and courageous. And in whatever way is right for you, just allow this gift to emerge and present itself to you in its own natural time and way. And when it does, now, you will know with an inner certainty that your journey has helped you connect with the highest expressing of your own deep wisdoming.

And as you continue to rest and sleep, protected by the tree, you may draw upon the power of life and nature, you may also draw the power of the earth up within you, to heal and renew you. Feel the wisdom and intuitive power flow like warmth, up from within the earth, into your body to soothe any pain, any tiredness, to give you strength and love and wholeness. Helping you to connect deep within your heart, mind and body, deep within your gut, aligning and integrating. Feeling the natural flow of life, feeling it deeply now, as you float free, at peace. Strong and whole...

1. FOR SLEEPING

And nestling in the forests embrace, you feel the power of life flowing like warmth, slowly, easily, up through your body, up through your mind. You are drifting, happy and serene. Your mind and body in harmony with nature. Protected and loved. Feel the strength and wisdom now, here, of the ancient tree as it draws the life-force up from the earth, to spread and share it with the world.

Feel the beauty of the world, the warmth of life. You are perfect and worthwhile. A beautiful part of this world. Deeply relaxed and floating, floating into a long and perfect sleep. An easy sleep, a good sleep. Deeper and deeper into a refreshing sleep. Knowing that you are safe and relaxed, at peace with the world. And you will sleep deeply now and not awaken until morning or until you are ready.

You will have a deep and uninterrupted sleep, and will not awaken until it is right and appropriate to do so. And when finally you awaken you will feel refreshed, alert and alive, feeling loved, whole and strong. Able and ready to face the world, happy and calm and full of boundless energy and life. Able to be the most compassionate, creative and courageous you that you can feel, be and do. And until you awaken you will sleep easily and deeply. You are calm and relaxed, floating, floating, deeper, deeper...

Sleep deeply and peacefully now...

2. TO END THE JOURNEY

And now, here, nestling in the forests embrace, you feel the power of life flowing like warmth, slowly, easily, up through your body, up through your mind. You are drifting in a dreamless sleep, happy and serene. Your mind and body in harmony with nature.

Around you fluffy white clouds begin to form. Soft, safe, warm fluffy whiteness. A world of creative opportunity. The white light of healing and generativity. A white canvas you can paint infinite possibilities on in your life.

And laying nestled in this world of white, you can allow your whole body to begin to relax even more deeply, now, starting from your toes and moving upwards. Picture your toes relaxing, and feel the relaxation flow like warmth from your toes through your feet. Relaxing your feet, and feeling the warmth spread from your feet to your ankles. Relaxing your ankles and legs, calves and knees, and feeling this wonderful warmth spread deeply into your calves and knees. This healing warmth spreads slowly upwards and inwards. You are lying relaxing in your forest, surrounded by a soothing blanket of whiteness, on this warm and comfortable day, safe deep in the heart of your world.

Relaxing so deeply and easily, joyfully and calmly... and as you relax your thighs and pelvis, hips and stomach, feel the warmth spread easily up into your body, into your torso. Feel the warmth and healing relaxation spread into your chest and up into your spine and back, into your shoulders and down into your arms, down into your hands...

You are lying on the relaxing grass, deep in your forest, so safely relaxed and calm. And as you continue to sink deeply into the grass, safe and at peace, you can lay here easily, safely. Feeling the peace of the silence, the peace of the space. Thinking nothing. Your mind so totally relaxing...

[Allow a couple of minutes of peaceful space.]

You are protected and loved. Feel the strength and wisdom of the ancient tree that keeps watch over you here in the heart of the forest. As it draws the wise life-force up from the earth, to spread through you and allowing you to compassionately share it with the world.

Feel the beauty of your world, the warmth of life. You are perfect and worthwhile. A beautiful part of this world. Deeply relaxed and floating, at the heart of your wonderful and amazing forest.

And when you are ready, and in your own good time, know that you can awaken easily now, open your eyes slowly and gently, stretch, take a deep, deep breath and return from the forest, feeling strong and alive, refreshed and full of boundless energy and love. Slowly you can return from the forest, feeling refreshed and alive. So when you are ready, now, gently open your eyes, stretch, breathe deeply, and feel awakened, alive and refreshed...

Happy and whole. Filled with life and wise energy now. And knowing deeply, truly and really that you will be able to bring a deep and ongoing sense of peace and calmnessing, of compassion, creativity and courage, to everything that you do, so that you will, from now on, here, continue to live into the highest expressing of your self in wise and wonderful ways.

Journey 3

FLOATING ON AN OCEAN WAVE...

[Read the following guided visualization script with a slow, gentle and mellifluous voice, allowing time for pauses and space for your Journeyer to breathe slowly and evenly in time with your voice and to go deep into the creativity of their own experience of your words.]

Begin now by finding a place to safely and gently relax...

Start by taking a deep easy breath and quietly, calmly and slowly begin to center your mind and center your self... Take a deep, deep breath and slowly exhale any tension from your body and your mind.

Here, now, as you listen easily to the sound of my voice, allow yourself to calmly begin to drift off. And as you do, begin also to gently and easily breathe in and breathe out, in a balanced, even, easy way... So that your in-breath and out-breath are of the same equal duration. Breathing approximately 6-seconds in, and 6-seconds out.

And as you continue to breathe, easily and evenly, calmly and gently, allow your beautiful attention to come slowly into the region of your heart, so that with every breath, you are deeply and effortlessly breathing a sense of peace and calm and ease into the region of your beautiful heart…

And as you continue to breathe, calmly and effortlessly, easily and evenly, allow this beautiful, gentle sense of ease, peace and wellness to begin to expand from your heart up into your head. With each in-breath up from your heart to your head, and slowly, slowly, gently, easily on each out-breath down deep into your beautiful gut… Your mind calming, your belly softening. Breathing in ease and calming peace, breathing out any tension from your body. Breathing in peace, breathing out tension. Breathing peace into your heart, breathing wonderful calm deep down into your gut.

And here, now, as you continue to breathe so easily and peacefully, begin also to gently relax your muscles in your body starting from your feet and moving upwards. You can easily allow the muscles of your feet to become relaxed, relaxing so easily, and with each balanced breath that you are taking, you might allow yourself to feel your feet becoming even more loose, comfortable and more deeply relaxing. Breathing in soooo deeply, breathing out soooo easily… It is natural to relax, all natural, to let yourself relax, your body relaxing, your mind calming and at ease…

And allow yourself to let this beautiful sense of relaxation begin to spread to your calves… you might notice your calves are becoming warm, heavy and relaxed, the muscles smoothing out, softening, relaxing easily and completely letting go. You can feel this easily and deeply. A deep sense of relaxing peace moving from your feet to your calves.

And this delicious warmth can begin spreading from your calves to your thighs, gently allowing your relaxing attention to concentrate so easily and effortlessly into this beautiful spreading, warm feeling in your legs, as you sooo easily continue to breathe in airs of relaxation, and breathing, now, gently, out airs of any residual tensing, inhaling calm, exhaling peace, easily and effortlessly... Noticing how your legs are wonderfully relaxing now, here, warm and heavy, as you hear the sound of my voice, as it washes over and through you and allows your conscious mind to calmly and gently concentrate or not, on the good feelings of deeply relaxing in your legs, your legs feeling so very loose and so relaxed, heavy and supported, calmly being, deeply relaxing, as you so very deeply and truly enjoy the calm feelings of relaxation in your legs for a moment or two...

And now, in your own time, relaxing here, begin to allow your wonderful sense of relaxation to spread from your legs into your buttocks and pelvic area... you might begin to feel your hips settle, the muscles softening and relaxing. As you get a deep, deep sense of inner peace, that allows you to begin relaxing even more deeply now, and as you do, just notice how your sense of peace and relaxation spreads deeper and deeper into your gut and abdomen.

Relaxing every organ in your gut. Letting your sense of peace flow deeply within. Easily relaxing your gut and abdomen, and now relaxing your back, every muscle in your back gently becoming so very relaxed, at ease, loose and wonderfully comfortable now...

And you might allow this deep sense of relaxation to spread along your spine and up into your chest, into your shoulders, feeling the warmth and heaviness as your body settles into whatever surface supports you now. And as you do, allow your wonderful calming sense of relaxation to travel into your hands, your relaxing arms and hands, allowing them to become even more relaxed and limp, without tension, free, natural, easy, calm...

With your arms heavy at your side, warm, loose and relaxing... gently open your mouth slightly, your lips gently part and let the muscles of your mouth relax. Your tongue soft, your jaw loose, relaxing your entire face, easily, calmly, lovingly. Your eyes gently relaxed and floating in their sockets, so deeply relaxing, your eyelids heavy and relaxing, any residual tension draining out of your face. Your face smoothing out, relaxing, softening, calming. Your temples and forehead so smooth, calm and so relaxed...

Your face is smooth, unwrinkled, calm. A deep sense of peace and calm, that with every breath, you feel flowing from your heart and gut up to your face and deeply into your wonderful head... Allowing your mind to relax, letting it be free, floating. Your body sinking heavily, easily into the relaxing surface that is supporting you now, so relaxed, your mind free, at ease and floating gently in this deep sense of relaxing peaceful now...

You are deeply, deeply relaxed, truly really calm. Your mind is smooth, unwrinkled, calm. Your body is at ease. You are safe. You are at peace in your heart, at peace deep within your mind, at peace deep, deep within your body. The relaxation is all through you, and so is the calm that goes with it, the calm of it is part of you, it is all through your heart, gut and body and all through your mind…

Your calm pervades you, you let yourself go with it, you let yourself go more and more completely, with each breath you let yourself go, and as you do, you let go of your breath, allowing it to be automatic and easy, you are deeply relaxing, calming, floating, nothing matters, nothing else matters. Just you at ease and at peace…

And as this wonderful sense of ease and inner peace flows through and within you, with every even, easy breath… now, here, let us begin once more to go even deeper and deeper into a joy filled and delightful inner journey… an ocean journey… a journey of easily guided visualization, where you can follow along or not, as most deeply suits you, and allow the imagery and deep sensory experience to unfold with delight, or as you prefer, in whatever way works for you, just allow my voice, here, now, to flow around you as you consciously drift off, beautifully and easily…

And now… I want you to simply, slowly and easily begin to imagine yourself standing high upon a beach. High upon the dunes. Standing easily on the majestic dunes, looking gently down.

Before you stretches mile upon endless mile of rolling breaker and golden white sands. Beautiful. And oh so peaceful… Settling your mind, awakening your senses, calming your spirit…

The straight, straight line of the horizon, unbroken and so distinct from the deep blue green of the sea, divides the world in two. This is nature's art, nature's canvas. It is a beautiful sight… It fills your heart with delight. You can feel this deeply now…

And as you do, you might begin to notice that a golden warming sun drenches this beauty filled landscape, glistening on sand crystals, throwing minute shadows from its position overhead.

Around you, golden green grasses top the sheltered dunes and waver in the gentle breeze that is sweeping down the sand, bringing a moist, clean, salty fragrance. A healing fragrance that you can taste on your skin, taste in your lungs. The smell of the sea with hints of salt and seaweed. The taste of cleansing, healing salt on your tongue. And you might begin to gently feel the air's warm and relaxing caress on your skin. Gently. Deliciously. Relaxingly.

And in the sky, you can see now, a pale ghost of a large full moon hangs languidly on the horizon. Gulls stand motionless, on guard at the water's edge, watching patiently. Protecting you. Their majestic white-washed feathers gleaming. You feel their love and protection. While you are here, they will bring you compassion and connection so that you know, while you are here, peacefully by yourself, and yet you are not alone, as your gulls and the moon watch lovingly over you. Sending your heart caring, kind energy…

And now, easily and effortlessly you begin to glide slowly down the dune to the beach below. Fine golden white sands, drift in sprays with the gentle wind on every footstep. You might notice now the feel of the sand caressing your feet, its silken fineness between your bare toes. Feel its soft, warmth and silken caress. And you can enjoy this deeply pleasuring feeling now…

Ahead, you may become aware of the rolling, surging breakers. A moving, flowing line of white and blue and green. Echoing soothingly in your ears. The sound of the surf and the wind's gentle call. And the deep and soothing sound, as the waves, releasing their energy to the land, come rolling, boiling, surging upon the warm sands, to recede with a sigh. Ebbing and flowing. Surging gently and deeply. A deep and satisfying sigh...

And you can notice the sound is strongest straight ahead, and constant and diminishing all around, cycling and in rhythm. The rhythm and flow of the tides of life. An easy change that reflects the impermanence of all things. A loving flow that brings life and reflects the deep compassion of a loving and caring world and universe. Here safely on your beach. Your mind perfectly at peace in a world of which you are a deep and valued part. Your own special self. Flowing like a wave onto the beach of your life...

And looking easily around, you might begin to see your imprints in the trackless sands, as you wander amongst small pools of pale, faded shells, pieces of mustard colored sponge and brown, scoured skerricks of driftwood. Interestingly, you can notice the shells and driftwood. Natures creative art. The small pieces of sponge and sea wrack. The pastiche of the treasure of the sea. A collage of color on a background of golden sand.

And you can take an easy moment now, to notice and explore this wonderful treasure of life that the sea provides. Always changing. Always so fascinating and beautiful. An adventure of shapes and colors. A delight to wonder just what you may find during this ocean journey… what may wash up from the wondrous depths onto the shore of your awareness…

And overhead you can see the deep blue sky, mother blue, healing, whole. Whilst across the horizon a small, solitary white cloud is happily wandering. Creativity at play.

The sun is streaming down, the breeze is warm, you are comfortable and relaxed. Deeply relaxing. Oh so deeply relaxing on this wonderful, peaceful and joy filled journey. And you can find yourself moving easily across the sand, down to the water's edge. At your feet, seaweed glistens wetly, streaked with foam. Waves gently washing the sand, like uneven tongues. Seagulls wheeling freely through the sky, in effortless play. Compassion and creativity in action.

Between each wave the surface of the water is filled with smaller wavelets and their echoes. Always moving, never still. Beautiful. Notice the play of the wavelets. The edges of the sea washing creamy white onto the sand, as wisps of spray are caught softly into the air by the warm and balmy breeze. And in the sunlight the spray making rainbows that come alive and then gently drift away.

Effortlessly and comfortably you move into the surf. The surging, rolling water is warm and relaxing, as it washes around and over your sun-drenched body. Feel the water washing warmly and soothingly against your skin. Feel the gentle surge and play of the waves around your body…

You are relaxing safely in the water now and can allow yourself, here, to begin to float out easily past the gentle breakers, to the crystal clear shallows beyond. The sea supports and caresses you, and with your eyes easily closing you drift, drift, floating, safely and at ease in this sea of warmth. Your arms floating easily at your sides, your lips gently parting, breathing even more softly and evenly as any residual tension drains from your body into the healing embrace of the sea. Ahhhhh.

[Allow a couple of minutes of peaceful space.]

The sun is shining overhead, you feel the warmth and life flowing through you. You feel the courageous energy of the ocean filling every cell within you. You are made of water like the sea, you have a deep evolutionary link to its power. Your body filled with gutsy courage, your heart filled with life giving compassion. Your head awash with incredible creativity and life. Your mind is free. You are drifting, drifting, naturally, free. Floating in a warm and gentle world of peace, strength, love and safety...

[Allow a couple of minutes of peaceful space.]

And as and when you are ready, gradually and easily you can begin now gliding back to shore. Slowly and easily returning to the shore. Your body slides and glides through the water. The waves gently tumble and roll around you, massaging your relaxed and supple body.

And slowly reaching the shore, you glide up upon the beach, and with a smile and a sigh, sink peacefully onto the warm golden white sand. Feel the sand's caress, supporting you gently, evenly, all over. Its warmth radiating deeply through you...

With your hands loosely at your sides, you sink and sift your fingers slowly and gently through the sand, and feel its soft resistance, the smoothness of its flow, as crystal slips over crystal, in a fine powdered fall. So soft, so smooth, so easy.

Laying relaxed, your eyes half closed and closing deeply and easily now, you feel the salt drying in patterns on your skin. Feel your skin drying deliciously. The warm taste of salty sea water on your lips. The taste of life and love. The healing smell of the sea filling your lungs with every deep, even, easy breath.

The sound of the gentle breeze, caressing your ears, distinct only between the heartbeat of the waves. Hear the slow and steady heartbeat of the waves. Like your own heartbeat, filled with deep compassion for yourself and all life.

Through your closing, heavy lids you barely see the dunes behind, like a wall of sand, protecting you from the world. Safe and protected. Nurtured and supported. Loved and valued... You lay, sinking even more heavily and easily into the soft and supporting sand, enveloped in the fragrance of sun and salt and sea. Safe, relaxed and happy.

And in the distance, the gentle call of sea birds gliding over the waves, hovering in the breeze. Their satisfied peep and 'gurrow'. You are slowly beginning to drift, floating, and now rising higher and higher like a bird yourself. Drifting and sailing up above the world, ranging gently and safely on the wind…

Far, far below, you can see the line of wave wet sand, wavering scallop edged into the hazy, salt swept distance. All white and blue, filled with echoes of mood and movement and a quiet nameless sound. An open canvas of creativity on which you can paint the dreams of your life purpose.

Higher and higher you soar. Gaining perspective. Rising freely on the wind. Floating, safely and easily. Connecting with an intuitive sense of wisdom as you see more and more of your world.

And now, here, you begin flying smoothly high across the sea, far above the opaque depths of the translucent water, like milky green crystal, and in the distance you can notice a narrow, white strip of beach, gently receding, gently receding away.

Moving through your azure sky, weightless and serene, banking and wheeling in effortless flight. You are travelling now over islands and lands of green and brown and gold, threaded with twisting streaks of blue grey streams. You can see the islands of green, brown and gold. And on and on over lands of forest all folded and valley green, drifting over fields of golden shimmering grain.

High, high above, gliding swiftly, you can easily rise up above rugged mountain ranges, majestic and strong. Timeless and everlasting. Gaining more and more wisdom as you traverse this world of your compassion, creativity and courage.

As onwards you travel, across horizons flat, bare and featureless, through deserts and gorges deep. Floating down easily, to skim dark flat lakes that mirror the golden sun, and up, up again through the safe fluffy whiteness of playful clouds to the warming blue of the clear azure sky above.

Until once again, the open sky and sea, a world of blue and green. You are soaring towards a tiny island of green, nestled upon the horizon, and drawing closer. Closer... Until you begin to see it ringed by coral reefs. Turquoise blue waves lapping upon golden sands, sparkling white foam, the spray washing back, like blond hair streaming in the wind, the waves casting shimmering wet rainbows of gentle mist as it drifts slowly down.

You can notice the air is warm and sweet with the scent of tropical fruit. Delicious. Warm and sweet. Long languid palms sway heavily. As you glide smoothly above the beach, banking and turning. Below in the sand, you see the wrinkled patterns of the tides long retreat, and beyond the shallows, wave overtaking slower wave, building the surge of blue.

And out on the reef, the barnacle and oyster encrusted rocks, brown granite colored, roughly smoothed and shaped by the ceaseless movement of the sea, washed by gentle waves. Surging and retreating. Surging and returning. The white foam, blue, clear dump of water on the rock now cascades off as the wave passes. Notice the waves cascading gently. Rising and falling. The seaweed washing fore and throw, tumbled, floating... While boiling behind each breakers demise, small turmoil'ed whirlpools creatively play...

And in amongst the rocks, you may notice deeper languid rock-pools. Filled with life. You can see, now, wonderfully colored corals, beautiful starfish, and small playful fish. All growing and living in the oceans rhythmic abundance. And you can take a moment now to deeply appreciate and enjoy the regenerative beauty you see before you as you look deeply into these life-filled pools...

And so, now, drifting and turning, light upon the tropical air, you gradually, so gradually return to the land, and sink peacefully and lovingly onto the sun warmed sand. You are drowsy and tired, safe upon this beautiful and wondrous tropical island. Relaxing deeply. Soaking in the energy and wisdom of the world...

Your head, heart and gut so deeply in synch with the rhythms and energy of life. Every cell in your body filled with wellness and vitality. Your mind, body and life filling with a deep sense of purpose. Compassionate purpose. Creative purpose. Courageous Purpose. Wise purpose...

And as you relax even more deeply into the beaches loving embrace, you may be wonderfully delighted to find that the ocean has a gift of treasure for you. From deep within its wise and powerful depths, it has something to share with you that will add value to your life. It may be a message, or an idea. It may be a wise, compassionate, creative and gently courageous suggestion or intuitive insight. And this treasure may come fully formed into your consciousness now, or it may naturally emerge over the coming minutes, hours or days. Like the ebb and flow of the tides and waves you can allow it to naturally emerge. And when it does, you will know that your ocean journey, connecting you to the deep sea of your wise and intuitive unconscious mind, from the deep alignment and the highest expressing of your heart, head and gut, has gifted you a treasure that helps you make a generative difference to your life and the world.

And so now, here, allowing the natural processes of unconscious treasuring to occur, you can continue delightfully relaxing deeply on the shore…

1. FOR SLEEPING

And nestling in the sands embrace, you continue to feel the power of life flowing like warmth, slowly, easily, up through your body, up through your mind. You are drifting, happy and serene. Your mind and body in harmony with nature. Protected and loved. Feel the strength and wisdom of the sea as it draws the life-force up from the earth, to spread and share it with you and the world. Mother ocean, giver of life.

Feel the beauty of the world, the warmth of life. You are perfect and worthwhile. A beautiful part of the world. Deeply relaxing and floating… floating into a long and perfect sleep. An easy sleep, a good sleep. Deeper and deeper into a refreshing sleep. Knowing that you are safe and relaxed, at peace and at ease. You will sleep deeply and not awaken until the time is just right.

You will have a deep and uninterrupted sleep, and will not awaken until you are ready. And knowing deep in your heart, mind and body that when you finally awake, you will awaken refreshed, alert and alive, feeling loved, whole and strong. Able and ready to face the world, happy and calm and full of boundless wisdom, energy and life. But until you awaken, you will sleep easily and deeply. You are calm and relaxed, floating, floating, deeper, deeper…

Sleep peacefully and easily now…

2. TO END THE JOURNEY

[Allow a couple of minutes of peaceful space.]

And nestling in the sands loving embrace, you feel the power of life flowing like warmth, slowly, easily, up through your body, up through your mind. You are drifting in a dreamless sleep, happy and serene. Your mind and body in harmony with nature.

Protected and loved. Feeling the strength and wisdom of the sea as it draws the life-force up from the earth, to spread and share it with you and the world. Mother ocean, giver of life, life's protector…

You can easily feel the beauty of the world, the warmth of life. You are perfect, valued and worthwhile. A beautiful part of the world. Deeply relaxing and floating, nestled by the sea. And when you are ready, and in your own good time, know that you can awaken easily, stretch, and return from this Ocean and Island haven, feeling strong and alive, full of boundless energy and love. Slowly you can return from the beach, feeling refreshed and deeply, deeply alive.

So that when you are ready, now, gently open your eyes, stretch, breathe deeply, and feel awake, alive and refreshed. Happy and whole. Here now. Returned here, now, full of passion and energy, life and love for your self and your world. Awake and alert. And knowing deeply, truly and really that you will be able to bring an ongoing sense of peace and calmnessing, of compassion, creativity and courage, to everything you do, so that you will, from now on, here, continue to live into the highest expressing of your self in wise and wonderful ways.

Journey 4

SAFE IN A PEACE-FILLED LOG CABIN...

[Read the following guided visualization script with a slow, gentle and mellifluous voice, allowing time for pauses and space for your Journeyer to breathe slowly and evenly in time with your voice and to go deep into the creativity of their own experience of your words.]

Begin now by finding a place to safely and gently relax...

Start by taking a deep easy breath and quietly, calmly and slowly begin to center your mind and center your self... Take a deep, deep, easy breath and slowly exhale any tension from your body and your mind...

Here, now, as you listen easily to the sound of my voice, allow yourself to calmly begin to drift off... And as you do, begin also to gently and easily breathe in and breathe out, in a balanced, even, easy way... So that your in-breath and out-breath are of the same equal duration. Breathing approximately 6-seconds in, and 6-seconds out.

And as you continue to breathe, easily and evenly, calmly and gently, allow your beautiful attention to come slowly into the region

of your heart, so that with every breath, you are deeply and effortlessly breathing a sense of peace and calm and ease into the region of your beautiful heart...

And as you continue to breathe, calmly and effortlessly, easily and evenly, allow this beautiful, gentle sense of ease, peace and wellness to begin to expand from your heart up into your head. With each in-breath up from your heart to your head, and slowly, slowly, gently, easily on each out-breath down deep into your beautiful gut... Your mind calming, your belly softening. Breathing in ease and calming peace, breathing out any tension from your body. Breathing in peace, breathing out tension. Breathing peace into your heart, breathing wonderful calm deep down into your gut.

And here, now, as you continue to breathe so easily and peacefully, begin also to gently relax your muscles in your body starting from your feet and moving upwards. You can easily allow the muscles of your feet to become relaxed, relaxing so easily, and with each balanced breath that you are taking, you might allow yourself to feel your feet becoming even more loose, comfortable and more deeply relaxing. Breathing in soooo deeply, breathing out soooo easily... It is natural to relax, all natural, to let yourself relax, your body relaxing, your mind calming and at ease...

And allow yourself to let this beautiful sense of relaxation begin to spread to your calves... you might notice your calves are becoming warm, heavy and relaxed, the muscles smoothing out, softening, relaxing easily and completely letting go. You can feel this easily and deeply. A deep sense of relaxing peace moving from your feet to your calves... And this delicious warmth can begin spreading from your calves to your thighs, gently allowing your relaxing attention to concentrate so easily and effortlessly into this beautiful spreading, warm feeling in your legs, as you soooo easily continue to breathe in airs of relaxation, and breathing, now, gently, out airs of any residual tensing, inhaling calm, exhaling peace, easily and effortlessly...

Noticing how your legs are wonderfully relaxing now, here, warm and heavy, as you hear the sound of my voice, as it washes over and through you and allows your conscious mind to calmly and gently concentrate or not, on the good feelings of deeply relaxing in your legs, your legs feeling so very loose and so relaxed, heavy and supported, calmly being, deeply relaxing, as you so very deeply and truly enjoy the calm feelings of relaxation in your legs for a moment or two...

And now, in your own time, relaxing here, begin to allow your wonderful sense of relaxation to spread from your legs into your buttocks and pelvic area... you might begin to feel your hips settle, the muscles softening and relaxing. As you get a deep, deep sense of inner peace, that allows you to begin relaxing even more deeply now, and as you do, just notice how your sense of peace and relaxation spreads deeper and deeper into your gut and abdomen...

Relaxing every organ in your gut. Letting your sense of peace flow deeply within. Easily relaxing your gut and abdomen, and now relaxing your back, every muscle in your back gently becoming so very relaxed, at ease, loose and wonderfully comfortable now.

And you might allow this deep sense of relaxation to spread along your spine and up into your chest, into your shoulders, feeling the warmth and heaviness as your body settles into whatever surface supports you now. And as you do, allow your wonderful calming sense of relaxation to travel into your hands, your relaxing arms and hands, allowing them to become even more relaxed and limp, without tension, free, natural, easy, calm…

With your arms heavy at your side, warm, loose and relaxing… gently open your mouth slightly, your lips gently part and let the muscles of your mouth relax. Your tongue soft, your jaw loosening, relaxing your entire face, easily, calmly, lovingly. Your eyes gently relaxed and floating in their sockets, so deeply relaxing, your eyelids heavy and relaxing, any residual tension draining out of your face. Your face smoothing out, relaxing, softening, calming. Your temples and forehead so smooth, calm and oh so relaxed…

Your face is smooth, unwrinkled, calm. A deep sense of peace and calm, that with every breath, you feel flowing from your heart and gut up to your face and deeply into your wonderful head… Allowing your mind to relax, letting it be free, floating. Your body sinking heavily, easily into the relaxing surface that is supporting you now, so relaxed, your mind free, at ease and floating gently in this deep sense of relaxing peaceful now…

You are deeply, deeply relaxed, truly really calm. Your mind is smooth, unwrinkled, calm. Your body is at ease. You are safe. You are at peace in your heart, at peace deep within your mind, at peace deep, deep within your body. The relaxation is all through you, and so is the calm that goes with it, the calm of it is part of you, it is all through your heart, gut and body and all through your mind... Your calm pervades you, you let yourself go with it, you let yourself go more and more completely, with each breath you let yourself go, and as you do, you let go of your breath, allowing it to be automatic and easy, you are deeply relaxing, calming, floating, nothing matters, nothing else matters. Just you at ease and at peace...

And as this wonderful sense of ease and inner peace flows through and within you, with every even easy breath... now, here, let us begin once more to go even deeper and deeper into a joy filled and delightful inner journey... a safe and peaceful journey... a journey of easily guided visualization, where you can follow along or not, as most deeply suits you, and allow the imagery and deep sensory experience to unfold with delight, or as you prefer, in whatever way works for you, to allow my voice, here, now, to flow around you as you consciously drift off, beautifully and easily...

And now... I want you to begin to simply and easily imagine that you find yourself in a dimly lit cabin. A log cabin. A safe and spacious cozy cabin, built with nurturing love. Take a deep, deep breath and slowly exhale with a soothing, calming sigh. You are safe. You are protected. You are surrounded by strong walls of peace and love. Take another deep breath, and as you exhale, feel any old residual tension dissolve, feel it flow out from within you.

You are in a safe and peace filled cabin in the bush. Your own comfortable and rustic log cabin on your own beautiful bush-land retreat. Built just for you. And you can notice there is gentle sunlight filtering in from outside through small windows high upon the walls...

And you may also begin to notice, now, that you are gently laying on a soft, luxuriant rug, deeply caressing and resilient under your relaxed and sinking weight. Gently, softly, safely, calming. Feeling now the softness of your body as it sinks even more deeply into the relaxing embrace of the rug.

Beside you is an open fire, its flickering tongues of flame, gently warming the room, providing a golden, wavering light. Shadows dance around the cozy room to the fires flickering call. The cabin is rough hewn from logs and through the open lattice of its ceiling beams you can see that it is roofed with cedar slats.

The air is scented with burning pine, from the large glowing logs in the stone fireplace, their wood curved and brilliant with heat. Flames dancing across the surface, leaping in tongues, small brilliant flashes of spark bursting safely and beautifully up towards the chimney. The temperature is just right. You are feeling delightfully comfortable…

You look around the room and notice the room has been beautifully decorated with all the things you like and that fit well with this rustic setting. And as you lay here on the rug, easily, languidly, you begin to hear the sound of rain on the roof, a lovely refreshing sound. Its gentle drumming is even more calming now. You know deep inside that the rain shower is washing the world clean. Washing away anything that isn't needed or wanted. Making your world fresh and anew.

And laying here in this world of comfort, this world of gentle relaxing sound, the fresh smell of rain in the air around you, the subtle and warming smell of the open fire. Warmed and made drowsy by the crackling fire. Drifting, drifting. Comfortable and with your heart filled with delight. You can luxuriate in the calmness of this space, the calmness of this time, here, now, for just a moment or two...

[Allow a couple of minutes of peaceful space.]

And as you are laying here, in your cabin, on your rug, so peacefully. Continuing to breathe so calmly and evenly. You may begin to notice that the rain is easing. It is beginning to clear. And hearing the last few drops on the roof, you stand gently up, stretch and with a deep curiosity in your heart and mind, make your way to the door so you can explore outside.

And here outside now, you see that you are in a bush-land valley. Your valley. Protected and made safe just for you. There are trees and bushes stretching out into the distance. You are in a world of calming green. And around you, you may notice there are beautiful water droplets on every blade of grass that lay at your feet, glistening like diamonds... a field of scintillating jewels surrounding you in this glade that your cabin is nestled in... Take a moment to revel in the beauty of your jewel-filled wonderland.

And in the sky above you, a wondrous bright rainbow arcs across the heavens and brings beauty and wisdom, bridging the space between heaven and earth. It is a sign of hope and harmony. And if you go deep within, you may notice and feel its loving connection into your heart, and deep into your gut, and deeper even down into your pelvic floor. The rainbow's spectrum of beauty delights your senses and evokes a deep experience of spiritual wisdom into your mind and space...

In the trees around you, the sound of birds, as they fly playfully from tree to tree, keeping you loving company. Your heart connecting to them and filling even more with delight and joy. The sky is now clearing fully, turning a beautiful deep azure blue. Only a last few small clouds drifting lazily overhead. The sun shining brightly, a gentle, gentle breeze caressing your skin. The air tastes clean, clear, fresh. The smell of cleansing rain lingering. You feel alive, wonderful, in joy and at peace.

And along with the birds, you are kept company by a small, soft, playful furry animal that is calmly foraging around the glade. It is exploring under bushes, around the base of trees, and around the edges of rocks that you notice are interspersed amongst the grasses in your glade. This playful companion will quietly keep you company as it knows you are safe and it trusts you deeply and completely...

And over on one side of the glade, you notice a path that leads towards a small babbling stream. The stream runs from rocks higher up on the valley floor, in the distance, bubbling up crystal clear from the living earth. It comes from a permanent spring that brings life-giving water to your beautiful bush-land valley. It represents the deeply compassionate love of the earth for all life that it nurtures and supports. And as the stream turns and twists down the valley, you notice that ahead, in the direction of the path, there is a small lake or pond, filled with the crystal clear water. Providing a permanent source of calm, deep, beauty. The well-springs of full-hearted compassion.

So gliding onto the path, you find your way easily to where the stream enters the lake. Its waters flowing down a small waterfall, splashing ever so gently into the lake. The burbling flowing sound so restful and rejuvenating. See now the beauty of the ever flowing water, creating new patterns, constantly changing. The light from the sun reflecting and refracting in the ebb and flow of its changing form…

And easily, you bend down and cupping your hands, take some of the flowing crystal-clear, life-giving water and sip it. It is soooo refreshing and quenching. It tastes delicious. It tastes of life. As you easily swallow the crystal clear water you can feel it flowing from your mouth down deep into your gut, carrying its life-restoring goodness down deep inside. The water fills your body with love and energy and vitality. Liquid compassion. Flowing from the earth… these are healing spring waters. And you can feel them bringing health, love and wellness to every single cell in your body. Ahhhhh. So healing. So refreshing…

And now, gliding over to the edge of the lake, you notice that its surface is smooth and unrippled, like a giant mirror. Still and untroubled. Calm and glisteningly reflective. And as you peer into the mirror-like surface, you begin to see yourself reflected wonderfully. You can begin to look with compassion into your own eyes. See yourself reflected with love back to yourself…

And with this realization, you can also begin to see yourself in a deeper way, with the wisdom of the living waters and the deeper connected earth helping you to see how you are so deeply and compassionately connected to all living things, to all people, to all sentient beings. As you look deeply into your own eyes, your own soul, seeing yourself with a gentle deeper aligned wisdom. Feeling a heart to heart connection with yourself and all life. Feeling a deep gut to gut resonance with the world. Sensing a co-creative bond with all intelligence in the Universe. You know with certainty that all is well deep within your world.

And as you look even deeper now, below the surface, you notice an ancient wise fish. Its scales glinting and flashing silver as it slowly and gracefully moves across the bottom of the pool. Beautiful. Gentle poetry in languid motion. This ancient venerable fish has lived here since time untold, and it brings to you a sense of regeneration, of life sustained and renewed. It lives lovingly renewed, enriched and continuously enheartened through the power of the living water and the earth, which you have also now shared deep inside. And because of this you can feel a deep connection with this venerable soul and allow its deeper ways of meaning and wisdom to resonate gently into your own inner being.

Restfully, now, over to one side, you can begin to see, beside the pond, there is a strong, secure, rock. A rock made in a shape and size that seems just right for you to sit upon. It is a deeply meditative rock, that calls to you to come sit, come meditate… come rest in its strong courageous embrace. So easily you glide over to the rock, beside the deeply reflective waters of the lake, and taking a comfortable seat, you begin a short meditation.

You are sitting in a way that is at ease, and with a peace filled flow. Become aware now of how your shoulders are feeling, how your back is feeling, and if there's any sense of holding these or effort and just let that go and bring ease into your posture. You give your body a small wriggle to let any last residual tension go. So that the weight of your head is held naturally, with balance through your spine, evenly. Sitting in balance.

And begin, now, to take your attention ever inward. And just notice within yourself using your exquisite sense of inward attending. And you can be curious, just start by being curious and noticing... how your breath is entering your body. And know you don't need to change or do anything with it, just notice it. And follow your breath down as it goes to the back of the nose or throat and turns easily down to the lungs. And again just noticing where the air goes into the lungs, how deep into the lungs it goes.

As you are in this beautiful flowing mindfulness process, notice any sensations going below down deep into your lungs. Feel any sensations down deep into your diaphragm. You may notice the feelings of your chest expanding, your belly expanding, your diaphragm dropping. No need to change anything. Just awarenessing. Pure awarenessing. Without judgment. With simple equanimity. Just being mindful as you notice the inner sensations in your body with your deeply meditative breathing.

And as you let each breath out, you may now be aware of the air leaving you. Is it warmer as it leaves than it came in? Notice any sensations as the air flows out of your lungs, out of your nose or mouth. Out of your body. Simply noticing and being aware of the flow and inner sensations of your breathing. Noticing your in-breath to out-breath durations. Not changing anything consciously. Just letting your system and your wonderful autonomic and unconscious mind do what it does best. Bringing mindfulness to the natural process of sitting, meditating and breathing.

And as you allow your system to continue breathing, evenly and easily, naturally, safely on your meditative rock, under a deep blue sky, beside your calm reflective pool, begin to shift and expand your awarenessing, your consciousnessing, deeper inside into your heart-space. Let a little of your attention stay on your breathing, so you stay in natural rhythm. And allow your inner awareness to expand into your heart. And just notice, notice where you feel the beat and the rhythm of your heart...

Notice the quality of the beat. The sounds and feelings of your beautiful heart beat. Notice how it feels to be aware of your heart beat, your heart rhythm. And notice how it keeps beating even when you are not aware of it. And just be attentive to your compassionate loving heart and any messages it has for you now. How does it feel? How does your heart feel knowing that you are focused in the heart, with the heart. And just enjoy sensing your heart in this mindful way.

Start to notice how far out around you, your heart energy extends. Can you feel it at the top of the chest, up the sides of your neck, up into your scalp? And notice from your heart down into your torso, into your gut, into your pelvis. Become aware of any feeling of your heart beat down into your legs, down into your toes, out to your arms, down to your hands. And as you allow your beautiful heart to keep beating in just that right way and just that right wise rhythm for you…

Begin to drop your attention, your awareness, your consciousnessing down deep into your beautiful and gently courageous gut. What do you notice now, here? What comes into your deeper awarenessing? Is there any movement? Any sounds or gurgling? Any areas of tension or pressure? Warmth or tingling? Any messages or sense of importance from your gut, without specifically asking, just noticing what arises. Making no judgments. Just noticing. Just listening and connecting deep within…

Allowing the deep mindfulness of your gut to arise in your awareness. And you can scan around your torso and gut region, into your stomach, down to your liver, your pancreas, into your kidneys, down deep into your intestines, deeper even into your bowels, and even lower into your sexual or pelvic center. Just noticing. Making no judgment whatsoever. Simply allowing your inner intelligence to communicate whatever wisdom or message it wants or needs to…

And as you are easily and deeply feeling into this, just allow any feelings and signals to arise, to be and to be mindfully noticed. With calmness. Mindfully being in your gut, in your heart, in your body, in your bones, in your skin. Whatever you notice, just notice, and move on. You don't have to do anything with it, just allow it to be noticed and accepted. And as you move on, allow all your organs and systems to just continue to do what they are doing and are doing wonderfully and wisely well.

And now begin to move your attention, to expand your attention up to your amazingly creative head. And again just be aware in your head to simply notice what you notice. Without judgment. If there's any story in your head, just acknowledge it and drift away from it. If there are any words, thoughts, images, sounds, just notice them and allow them to move on. And maybe notice what's in the space of your head. The space where maybe you moved over quickly but where there's gems and pearls of wisdom, just notice those wisely creative ideas and calmly move your awareness on.

And now expand and flow your mindfulnessing and awarenessing back to your heart, and focus once again on your beautiful heart beat and rhythm. Recognizing and appreciating that it's beating throughout your whole body, sending signals into your high fidelity sensorium of all of your nerves and bodily intelligence, and beyond, outside of your body and into the space around you. Radiating energy and compassionate, creative and courageous love out into the world.

And now, here, when you are ready, bring your awareness back to your breathing. Gently and easily. Mindful of the air moving in and out of your body and lungs. Recognizing again where you are breathing from. The quality of the air and movement. And maybe take a refreshing deep breath in and allow the energy of the air, to give you vitality and love throughout your mind and body.

And so... smelling once again the freshness of the air, sitting easily on your meditative rock, beside a deep pool of regenerative wisdom. And coming back with full conscious attention to your presence in your safe and protected bush-land valley. Back beside your lake, kept company by the wise ancient fish and the birds at play in the trees and with the feeling of the sun on your skin, the gentle breeze in your hair, and now noticing all this with an added sense of multi-mindfulness presence. Look around. You are here, now, safe, energized and connected to a deeper wisdoming…

And so now, gently standing, stretching, you begin to easily flow back along the path, returning to your cabin. Moving past rocks and grasses, small bushes and shrubs. Nature's creativity in the artistic pageant of color and texture. A palette of greens and earthy browns…

With ease and grace you soon now find yourself back at your log cabin. Its sight fills you with a deep sense of peace and gratitude. And opening the door you move once again deeper inside. It is warm and inviting. Your rug comfortably beckons. You feel a languid feeling of relaxation spreading from your solar-plexus, gently radiating through every cell. So you lay once again down on your welcoming and loving rug.

1. FOR SLEEPING

And nestling in the rugs embrace, you continue to feel the gentle power of life flowing like warmth, slowly, easily, up from the earth, up through the floor of the cabin, up through your body, up through your mind. You are drifting, happy and serene. Your mind and body in harmony with life and nature. Protected and loved. Feeling the strength and wisdom of your wonderful log cabin as it draws the life-force up from the earth, to spread and share it with you and through you out into the world.

Feel the beauty of the world, the warmth of life. You are perfect and worthwhile. A beautiful part of the world. Deeply relaxing and floating... floating into a long and perfect sleep. An easy sleep, a good sleep. Deeper and deeper into a refreshing sleep. Knowing that you are safe and relaxed, at peace and at ease. You will sleep deeply and not awaken until the time is just right.

And while you sleep, your wonderful unconscious mind, your deeply compassionate heart, your gently courageous gut and your brilliantly creative head, can all work wisely together to bring to you a generative dream. A dream that has a message of wisdom for you. A dream that helps you connect with your deeper purpose. A dream that can bring to your life the seeds of personal evolution and help you begin to live the life that truly, really, deeply brings your human spirit alive.

And know that even while you dream, you will have a deep and uninterrupted sleep, and will not awaken until you are ready. And knowing deep in your heart, mind and body that when you finally awake, you will awaken refreshed, alert and alive, feeling loved, whole and strong. Able and ready to face the world, happy and calm and full of boundless wisdom, energy and life. But until you awaken, you will sleep easily and deeply. You are calm and relaxed, floating, floating, deeper, deeper...

Sleep peacefully and easily now...

2. TO END THE JOURNEY

And nestling in the rugs loving embrace, you continue to feel the gentle power of life flowing like warmth, slowly, easily, up from the earth, up through the floor of the cabin, up through your body, up through your mind. You are drifting, happy and serene. Your mind and body in harmony with life and nature. Protected and loved. Feeling the strength and wisdom of your wonderful log cabin as it draws the life-force up from the earth, to spread and share it with you and through you out into the world.

Feel the beauty of the world, the warmth of life. You are perfect and worthwhile. A beautiful part of the world. Deeply relaxing and floating... floating now into a short, refreshing and perfect sleep. An easy sleep, a good sleep. Deeper and deeper into a refreshing sleep. Knowing that you are safe and relaxed, at peace and at ease...

And while you sleep, your wonderful unconscious mind, your deeply compassionate heart, your gently courageous gut and your brilliantly creative head, can all work wisely together to bring to you a generative dream. A dream that has a message of wisdom for you. A dream that helps you connect with your deeper purpose. A dream that can bring to your life the seeds of personal evolution and help you begin to live the life that truly, really, deeply brings your human spirit alive...

And in this wise and wonderful dreaming, your beautiful heart can calmly tell you what it truly feels, desires, values and connects with. Your amazing head brain can show you what it really makes meaning of and perceives. And your courageous gut can inform you of what it deeply needs for you to be you and what you need to do and not do and are moved and motivated by.

So dream easily, wisely and peacefully now...

[Allow a couple of minutes of peaceful space.]

And now, here, protected and loved. Allowing the dream to continue to unfold in your unconscious mind so that over the days to come it can emerge a deeper wisdom into your unfolding conscious awareness and into your life. And feeling the strength and wisdom of the earth as it draws the life-force up from deep within, to spread and share it with you and the world...

You can easily feel the beauty of the world, the warmth of life. You are perfect, valued and worthwhile. A beautiful part of the world. Deeply relaxing and floating, nestled in your own log cabin, in your own bush-land retreat. And as your wonderful Journey comes to a close, and when you are ready, and in your own good time, know that you can awaken easily, stretch, and return from this bush-land haven, feeling strong and alive, full of boundless energy and love. Slowly you can return from the cabin, feeling refreshed and deeply, deeply alive.

So that when you are ready, now, gently open your eyes, stretch, breathe deeply, and feel awake, alive and refreshed. Happy and whole. Here now. Returned here, now, full of passion and energy, life and love for your self and your world. Awake and alert. And knowing deeply, truly and really that you will be able to bring an ongoing sense of peace and calmnessing, of compassion, creativity and courage, to everything you do, so that you will, from now on, here, continue to live into the highest expressing of your self in wise and wonderful ways.

Appendix - About NLP and *m*BIT

*m*BIT — multiple Brain Integration Techniques

As you probably know, *m*BIT is an exciting new coaching, leadership and personal evolution field, based on startling new insights into human intelligence and wisdom. Over the last decade or so, research in the field of Neuroscience has uncovered that we have complex, adaptive and functional neural networks, or *'brains'*, in our heart and gut regions. Called the cardiac and enteric brains respectively, these neural networks exhibit memory, intelligence and adaptive processing — they learn, change and adapt. For example, with around 500 million neurons in the gut, (about the size of a cat's brain), the enteric brain is able to perform a number of vital functions and competencies that go way beyond mere digestion. And not surprisingly this explains why we intuitively know that we have a *'gut wisdom'* that we ignore often at our peril.

The Developing Brains

It's interesting to note that the heart and gut brains are primal in both an evolutionary sense and a developmental sense. The gut brain for example evolved long before the head brain, and can be found in organisms such as sea slugs, sea cucumbers and spineless helminthes (a type of parasitic worm).

Fascinatingly, the development of our brains during gestation mirrors evolutionary sequencing. As the fetus begins to grow, cells form that will eventually become the various brains. A neural plate first forms and then rolls into a neural tube. This tube eventually becomes the spinal column and goes on to generate the cephalic head brain. However, at the point where the edges of that neural plate meet an out-poaching called the neural crest forms and this develops and begins the process of generating the gut brain as the crest derived cells colonize the developing gut. So before the neural tube has elongated and rolled up to form the encephalon and ultimately the complete head brain, the gut brain has already begun forming and populating the visceral region. Along the way, as the neural tube develops there is another out-poaching of what ultimately becomes the vagus nerve system and this forms the cardiac plexus and the innervation of the heart.

Dr. Michael Gershon is one of the leaders in the newly emerging field of neurogastroenterology, and has published a ground-breaking book entitled, 'The Second Brain: Your Gut Has a Mind of Its Own'. Dr. Gershon's book is being hailed as "a quantum leap in medical knowledge" and that it provides "radical new understandings about a wide range of gastro-intestinal problems." Gershon and his colleagues have shown that the enteric brain sends and receives nerve signals throughout the chest and torso and that it innervates organs as diverse as the pancreas, lungs, diaphragm and liver. The gut brain is also a vast chemical and neuro-hormonal warehouse and utilizes every class of neurotransmitter found in the head brain. According to Dr. Gershon over 80 percent of the serotonin used throughout the body and brain is made in the gut. Diseases of the head brain also affect the neurons in the gut and heart brains. Patients with Alzheimer's and Parkinson's diseases often suffer from constipation due to the same damage to their gut brains as is occurring in their cranial brains.

Neuroscience meets Ancient Wisdom

Yes, the heart and gut have their own deep intuitive intelligence and what's amazing is that we've known about this for thousands of years. Now finally science is catching up and validating what wisdom traditions have been saying for millennia. Indeed, in a review of the last 100 years of ethnographic data on spiritual traditions, researchers Frecska, Moro and Wesselman (2011) found that a tripartite concept of soul was the rule rather than the exception in aboriginal spiritual traditions, with the three *'souls'*, or intelligences, typically imbued in the head, heart and gut.

So yes, we have three brains, and each of them brings to life its own form of intelligence and its own set of prime functions and core competencies. Your multiple brains also communicate with one another, and can be aligned or not-aligned. Using methodologies from NLP (Neuro Linguistic Programming), Cognitive Linguistics and Behavioral Modeling, (more on this coming up) and informed by the latest Neuroscientific discoveries, the field of *m*BIT has codified a powerful system for communicating with and integrating the wisdom and intelligence of your multiple brains. I've written about this in detail in my book *'mBRAINING — Using your multiple brains to do cool stuff'*, and you can find out more details at my website www.mbraining.com.

As one of the original co-developers of this exciting new field of *m*BIT, I am well placed to share the insights it brings to human creativity, wisdom and happiness. We all know what it's like to have our head saying one thing, our heart another and our gut screaming out, *"Warning, warning, warning!"* In the work on *m*BIT, we found that wisdom requires alignment of the three brains and that the neural networks need to be operating in what is known as an *'Autonomically Balanced Mode'* (we'll get into this in more detail shortly). When these conditions aren't met, and our brains are in conflict, we end up sabotaging our own success and happiness. We make un-wise decisions, we aren't able to motivate ourselves, and we make mistakes that we end up regretting.

On the other hand, when all our brains are aligned and working together, when we are operating from a balanced and calm mode, our life runs smoothly, we bring innate and intuitive wisdom to our decisions, and our human spirit comes alive. This is the power of *m*BIT and *m*BRAINING.

*m*BIT Prime Functions

What *m*BIT uncovered is that each brain has a fundamentally different form of intelligence; they utilize different languages, have different goals and operate under different criteria. In other words, your head, heart and gut have different ways of processing the world, communicating, operating and addressing their own concerns and domains of expertise.

Our findings indicate that there are three core Prime Functions for each of the three brains:

HEART BRAIN PRIME FUNCTIONS

- **EMOTING** — emotional processing (e.g. anger, grief, hatred, joy, happiness etc.)

- **VALUES** — processing what's important to you and your priorities (and their relationship to the emotional strength of your aspirations, dreams, desires, etc.)

- **RELATIONAL AFFECT** — your felt connection with others (e.g. feelings of love/hate/indifference, compassion/uncaring, like/dislike, etc.)

GUT BRAIN PRIME FUNCTIONS

- **CORE IDENTITY** — a deep and visceral/bodily sense of core self, and determining at the deepest levels what is 'self' versus 'not-self'

- **SELF-PRESERVATION** — protection of self, safety, boundaries, hungers and aversions

- **MOBILIZATION** — motility, impulse for action, gutsy courage and the will to act

HEAD BRAIN PRIME FUNCTIONS

- **COGNITIVE PERCEPTION** — cognition, perception, pattern recognition, etc.

- **THINKING** — reasoning, abstraction, analysis, synthesis, meta-cognition etc.

- **MAKING MEANING** — semantic processing, languaging, narrative, metaphor, etc.

The importance of this to the realm of wisdom in life is two-fold. First, it's crucial when making decisions and taking action in life that all three intelligences are accessed and incorporated into the process. Without the head intelligence, things will not have been properly thought through and analyzed. Without the heart intelligence, there won't be sufficient values-driven emotional energy to care enough and prioritize the decision against competing pressures, or to take into account the impact on others. Without the gut intelligence there will not be adequate attention to managing risks nor enough willpower to mobilize and execute the decision once challenges arise.

The second implication for happiness and wisdom is that you need to ensure that you are not using one brain to do the function of another. Each brain has its own domain of competence and therefore is not the most competent in the other prime functions. This mistake can be typically seen in people's lives where they use their head brain to logic their way into a relationship decision that their heart brain doesn't truly care about, or the head brain is used to design goals and action plans that the gut brain just doesn't fully engage with.

Understanding the ANS

As hinted at above, the Autonomic Nervous System (ANS) is an important component in how your brains work together. The ANS innervates and connects with each of your brains and influences their overall mode of processing. So it's imperative to understand something about the ANS and how it works.

Your overall nervous system has two major divisions, the Voluntary and the Autonomic. The Voluntary System is mainly concerned with movement and sensation. The Autonomic Nervous System on the other hand is responsible for control of involuntary and visceral bodily functions. The functions it controls include:

- Cardiovascular
- Respiratory
- Digestive
- Urinary
- Reproductive functions
- The body's response to stress

It's called 'autonomic' because it is operates largely automatically and outside of conscious control. It's divided into two separate branches — the Sympathetic and Parasympathetic. These two branches work in a delicately tuned, reciprocal and (usually) opposing fashion. Simplistically, the Sympathetic system can be considered to be the *'fight or flight'* system. It allows the body to function under stress and danger.

The Parasympathetic system is the *'feeding and fornicating'* and *'rest and repose'* arm. It controls the vegetative functions of feeding, breeding, rest, recuperation and repose. The Parasympathetic system also typically provides ongoing opposition to the Sympathetic system to bring your total system into balance or homeostasis. Where the Sympathetic system is like the accelerator of a car, the Parasympathetic is akin to the brake.

In times of danger or stress, the Sympathetic system, which has a very fast onset and response, kicks in and gets you moving to handle or resolve the situation. The typically slower acting Parasympathetic system begins to operate after the danger has passed, and brings you back to normalcy. Without the opposing function of the Parasympathetic system your body would stay amped up, burning energy and fuel and eventually exhaust itself.

The ANS and Your Multiple Brains

As highlighted above, it's crucial to know about the Sympathetic and Parasympathetic systems because they innervate and deeply influence the operating mode of the heart, gut and head brains. There are major connections between the head brain hemispheres, the heart brain, the gut brain and these Sympathetic and Parasympathetic arms of the ANS, and since the two ANS components typically work in opposing ways, the dominance of one or the other leads to very different modes of processing throughout our multiple brains.

For instance, Parasympathetic activity generally slows the heart, whereas Sympathetic activity accelerates it. In the gut, Parasympathetic activity enhances intestinal peristaltic movement promoting healthy digestion and elimination whereas Sympathetic activity inhibits such activity during times when physical exertion requires catabolic (energy) mobilization. The following are some of the main influences of the two systems:

Sympathetic Activation

Activation of the Sympathetic nervous system has the following effects:

- Dilates the pupils and opens the eyelids
- Stimulates the sweat glands
- Dilates the blood vessels in the large skeletal muscles
- Constricts the blood vessels in the rest of the body
- Increases heart rate
- Relaxes and opens up the bronchial tubes of the lungs
- Contracts the sphincter of the bladder and the bladder wall relaxes
- Shuts down and inhibits the secretions in the digestive system
- Can lead to involuntary defecation
- Is associated with Right Hemisphere activation and dominance in the head brain (and therefore concurrent style of cognitive and emotional processing)

Parasympathetic Activation

Activation of the Parasympathetic Nervous System has the following effects:

- Constricts the pupils
- Activates and increases the secretion of the salivary glands
- Decreases heart rate
- Stimulates the secretions of the stomach
- Constricts the bronchial tubes and stimulates secretions in the lungs
- Stimulates the activity of the gastro-intestinal tract
- Is involved in sexual arousal
- Is associated with Left Hemisphere activation and dominance in the head brain (and therefore concurrent style of cognitive and emotional processing)

You'll notice here that a powerful functional principle is in play. That is, two modes of *opponent processing* are operating for autonomic control across your total system. Consequently, your multiple brains can function in ways that are Sympathetic dominant, Parasympathetic dominant, or some combination of the two (and for more details on how these two systems can combine, see my book *'mBraining'*). The end result is that your Sympathetic and Parasympathetic systems dramatically affect how each of the Prime Functions of your multiple brains express themselves to create your subjective world, and in particular what happens when the two systems are operating in what is known as a coherent or balanced mode.

The Consciousness of Highest Expression

One of the many powerful models emerging from *m*BIT action research is that each of our brains has what is known as a *'Highest Expression'*. This is an emergent competency that represents the highest, most optimized and adaptive class of intelligence or competency of each brain. The Highest Expressions of each brain are:

- Head brain   — **Creativity**
- Heart brain   — **Compassion**
- Enteric brain   — **Courage**

What's crucially important is that these Highest Expressions are only accessed and activated when a person is in an optimal state of neurological balance, or what is defined as *'autonomic coherence'*. This is when the person is neither too stressed nor too relaxed, but is in a flow state. And it makes sense doesn't it, that unless someone is in a neurological flow state with all going well, their perceptions of any particular issue or situation along and their subsequent decision-making will likely be impaired.

For example, if your ANS is functioning in an overly Sympathetic (e.g. stressed) state, your perceptions and decision-making will typically default to reactive conditioning. Conversely, if your ANS is functioning in an overly Parasympathetic (e.g. apathetic, depressed or *'freeze response'*) state, you'll exhibit an inability or lack of desire to act, or at best make timid decisions. Whereas in an optimum state of autonomic balance you are able to bring a higher order of consciousness to your decision-making and consequent actions. The insights of *m*BIT are that the wisest forms of Highest Expression only occur when your ANS is in a balanced coherent mode.

The Highest Expressions are also naturally integrative. Each relies upon the others in order to express itself fully and wisely. In actual practice, these *'virtues'* are neurologically integrative by their very nature and when expressed together enable the emergence of a higher order level of consciousness and wiser way of being.

For example, courage without compassion can quickly turn to cruelty, belligerence or domination. Compassion on the other hand, without generative creativity is what the Buddhists call *'dumb compassion'*; it can quickly lead to *'shared misery'* and do more harm than good. Creativity that is not connected to courageous action is mere mental-masturbation; it generates great ideas but changes nothing in the world due to inaction or ineffective action. Alternately, courage without creativity can become bull-headedness and inflexibility, leading to courageous stupidity. Finally, compassion not channeled through a gutsy will-to-action helps nobody in any tangible way. So each Highest Expression of the three brains only fully express wisely into the world when all three brains are aligned and working together.

Controlling your Autonomic Mode — Balancing the ANS

When a nurse or medical practitioner measures your heart rate, they typically count the number of pulses over a period of 15 seconds and then multiply by 4 to get the average number of beats per minute. They might then write on your chart that your heart is beating at say 76 beats per minute (bpm). But in reality it's almost never exactly at that average rate. Your heart is constantly speeding its rate up and slowing its rate down.

This is because, when your Autonomic system has Sympathetic dominance, your heart rate speeds up, and then as your Parasympathetic kicks in to bring the ANS back to homeostasis, your hear rate slows back down.

Heart Rate Variability (HRV) is the measure of the beat-to-beat changes that occur in your heart rate. Because of the links to the ANS and the effects that thoughts, feelings and impacts from the environment have on your multiple brains (head, heart and gut), your pulse rate and HRV are affected by all of these. Researchers have found that HRV is a very useful measure of how you and your heart are coping with stress and what sort of state your ANS and brains are in. The graph below shows the heart rate of a person who is under stress.

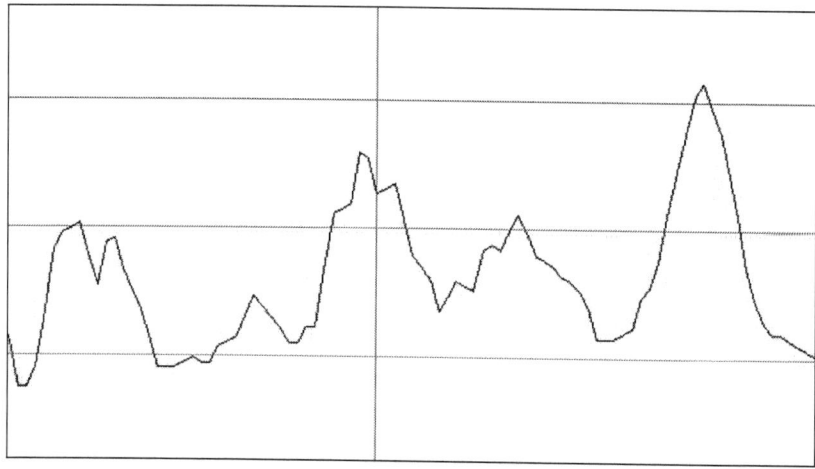

Contrast this with the one below from someone who is meditating and in a calm state, where they are focusing on feelings and thoughts of compassion and loving-kindness. Notice how smooth and even the changes in the heart rate are for the calm state. The graph almost looks like a sine wave. This sine shaped graph is one that has 'high coherence'. Coherence is a mathematical measure that describes how evenly repeatable from moment to moment a wave-form is. A chaotic, sharply changing wave has low coherence, it is not evenly repeatable. In high coherence however, the Sympathetic and Parasympathetic systems are working nicely together, in balance, gently keeping your mind and body in an optimal state, and this shows in the smoothly changing wave.

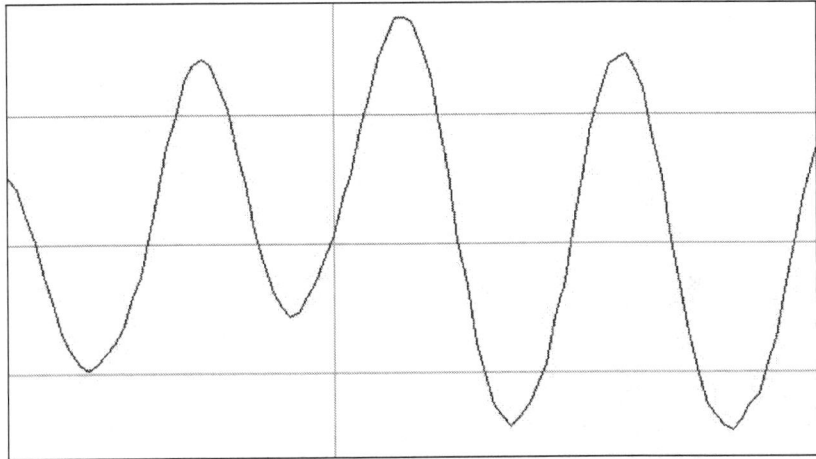

Numerous scientific studies have found that low HRV is one of the leading indicators of heart disease. They have also shown that high heart coherence is protective of the heart. Coherence acts to balance the heart, mind and emotions. It brings all the brains into resonance. When you are in a state of coherence you'll find you feel incredibly relaxed yet alert, your mind calms down and stress levels markedly decrease. It's a powerful state and one that is used for *m*BIT integration.

Resonant Breathing, Balanced Breathing

Breathing is primal and it's a powerful bridge between mind and body; the gateway between consciousness and the unconscious. In many languages the words for spirit and breath are identical. For example in Sanskrit the word is *'prana'*, in Hebrew *'ruach'*, Greek '*pneuma*', and Latin '*spiritus*'. Numerous ancient traditions such as those of the Native American Indians, also believe life enters the body with the first breath, not at the moment of birth or conception.

Breathing has direct and intimate connections to emotional states and moods. Take a look at someone who is angry, afraid or upset and you'll see a pattern of breathing that is shallow, rapid and irregular. Conversely, think about how you breathe when you are feeling happy, calm and contented. In fact, it's almost impossible to be upset if your breathing is slow, deep, gentle and regular. And there's a reason for this…

In part it's because your breathing is connected via the '*bridge*' of the diaphragm which is co-innervated by both somatic and enteric/autonomic nervous systems. It turns out that from an evolutionary perspective, the diaphragm can be viewed as two distinct muscles, the crural and costal, one a gastro-intestinal muscle and one a respiratory muscle. These two muscles typically act in synchrony during normal respiration, but diverge during swallowing and the reverse process of emesis (a fancy term for throwing up). The value in knowing this is that the diaphragm, being effectively two muscles in one, and therefore co-innervated by both the head and gut brains, is a powerful gateway between them.

Importantly, there's also another powerful physiological mechanism at work with breathing. This mechanism involves what is known as the '*baroreceptor reflex*' found in receptors in the carotid arteries. Deep in the sinuses of the large carotid arteries in your chest and neck, lay specialized neurons called baroreceptors. These cells are stretch-sensitive mechanoreceptors and are optimized for monitoring changes in blood pressure which they relay to the brainstem and ultimately, via the ANS, back to the heart.

The result of this is that as you breathe in, your blood pressure drops and the baroreceptors detect this and cause your heart rate to speed up. As you breathe out, your blood pressure increases and your heart rate slows down accordingly. In other words, through a complex process of information coding in the ANS, this baroreflex acts to speed up your heart as you breathe in and slow down your heart as you breathe out.

Why is this important? Well… it gives you a powerful gateway for controlling your Autonomic system and bringing your Sympathetic and Parasympathetic into balance and coherence. Via controlled, balanced breathing you can control the Sympathetic and Parasympathetic arms of the ANS through the baroreflex, and put your heart into high coherence.

Simply put, by breathing for an in-breath of approximately six seconds and an out-breath of exactly the same duration, the baroreflex, along with the co-innervation of the diaphragm, leads to coherence and balance in your ANS, and in your multiple brains. It all starts through conscious control of breathing, leads to the heart coming into resonance with the calm balanced breathing and this communicates and spreads to the gut and head brains all coming together into calm, balanced resonance with the heart.

Such a simple process, yet so powerful. And now you can see why breathing is linked to thoughts and emotions. When you alter your breathing, you profoundly alter the state and mode of processing of your ANS and your head, heart and gut brains.

Note also the importance of having a balance between the in-breath and out-breath. If you breathe longer on the in-breath, you'll cause a gradual speed up of your heart and shift into Sympathetic dominance. On the other hand, if you do lots of long sighs, that is, breathe longer on the out-breath compared to the in-breath, you'll end up slowing your heart down, and putting yourself into

Parasympathetic over dominance; another way of saying, you'll depress yourself.

These insights are obvious when you think about them. We've all had experiences of seeing someone panic and watching how they breathe when in that state. Similarly, you know when someone is depressed, they do lots of slow out-breath sighing. Start to notice this in yourself and others, and make sure you do balanced breathing to keep yourself in an optimal psychological and physiological state.

Generative Wisdom up the *m*BIT Roadmap

Ok, so you now know that you have three amazing brains, filled with deep intuitive intelligence, and they can be communicated with and brought into a balanced mode. You also know they can operate in what is known as their Highest Expressions and that when you do this it opens up greater levels of wisdom. But facilitating your multiple brains into alignment and getting them operating from their Highest Expressions requires a pragmatic '*how*' and some sort of suite of simple yet powerful techniques.

And this is what the field of *m*BIT is all about (and is detailed in my book '*mBraining*'), and is summarized in the diagram on the following page, known as the *m*BIT Roadmap.

In summary, the techniques and processes of *m*BIT involve getting into communication with your three brains, getting them aligned around any particular issue and then getting the brains functioning at their Highest Expression. When this is achieved, your innate intuitive wisdom emerges and the quality of your decisions and actions becomes adaptively and generatively different. The process is simple yet powerful.

Wisdom

Highest Expression

Creativity (cephalic brain)
Compassion (heart brain)
Courage (enteric brain)

Congruence

Communication

Throughout this book, as appropriate, we utilize aspects of these steps and processes. The techniques of *m*BIT have been incorporated into the Journeys and deeper guided unconscious explorations. And if you want to learn more then I highly recommend reading *m*BRAINING, or going on one of the transformational *m*BIT workshops that are run by skilled trainers across the world. You can find details of workshops and trainers near you at:

www.mbraining.com

Entraining Others

One last thing to share with you is that the state of your heart and your multiple brains doesn't just impact your own mind and body. Work by numerous researchers and organizations, and in particular by the Institute of Heartmath over the last 20 or more years, has shown that the electromagnetic signal of the heart extends strongly for many meters from each individual. And the signal has the ability to resonantly entrain other people's hearts and thereby their Autonomic state and the mode their multiple brains (head, heart and gut) are operating in.

Just like when you pluck say the E string on a guitar, a nearby instrument that is tuned to the same frequency, such as another guitar, violin etc. will begin to resonate in sympathy with the plucked string. So, in a similar way when you place yourself into Autonomic coherence and come from the Highest Expressions (of Compassion, Creativity and Courage) you are able to entrain and impact those around you and help them to more easily access these same generative states in their lives. Yes, happiness is contagious, just as is depression. This is why it's so very important to learn how to generate the Highest Expressions of happiness, wisdom and loving in your mind, body and life and thereby entrain and influence the people around you that you truly care for. Especially when facilitating someone on a guided Journey. This is how you create a life that is truly worth living and that brings your human spirit alive.

> *"Educating the mind without educating the heart is no education at all."*
>
> Aristotle

Neuro Linguistic Programming, Behavioral Modeling and Accelerated Learning

Over the last 40 years, Neuro Linguistic Programming (NLP) has been one of the fastest growing developments in applied psychotherapy. It is a technology of achievement and excellence, derived from studying how experts in different fields obtain their outstanding results. NLP provides models for human communication, learning and behavioral competence.

Science Digest reported that NLP, *"could be the most important synthesis of knowledge about human communication to emerge since the explosion of humanistic psychology... It may be the ultimate behavioral engineering tool."*

NLP provides a set of models, skills and techniques for thinking and acting effectively in the world, through which you can change, adopt or eliminate behaviors in yourself and others.

Another extremely powerful technology is Behavioral Modeling. This field provides processes for understanding, replicating and transferring expertise, abilities and skills. It can of course, be used to understand and codify such incredibly useful skills as creating and achieving meaning and happiness in life and loving yourself and your life more fully.

Accelerated Learning also presents popular and potent techniques for increased learning of new skills and knowledge. It is helping thousands of people around the world to learn more easily and effectively. Accelerated Learning reveals insights into how our memory functions and our brains best learn.

By combining and synthesizing the ideas and concepts and models from *m*BIT, NLP, Behavioral Modeling and Accelerated Learning, the *Journeys* in this book guide you through the processes, strategies and skills for unconsciously and generatively creating and amplifying more happiness, love and success in life.

This approach is based on modeling real-world expertise combined with scientific validity. In this way the guided visualization *Journeys for the Heart, Mind and Soul* in this book help you get results, providing you with a gentle yet pragmatic approach to living your life more fully and deeply.

Conscious and Unconscious Processes

In the field of Psychology there is still an active and ongoing debate about the Unconscious mind, its role, existence and structure. In NLP however there is an accepted model of the Unconscious mind that is largely being ratified by recent research in Cognitive Psychology.

In NLP, the Unconscious mind is seen as all of those processes that occur in the brain outside of consciousness. That is, the Unconscious mind can be thought of as the *'other-than-conscious'* mind. These are the processes for example that are responsible for brain and body functioning, for performing visual processing, for unconsciously directing attention and awareness. Thousands and thousands of both simple and complex processes and patterns, operating generally outside of your conscious awareness.

The noted Neuro-physiologist and psychologist, Robert Ornstein (1991) calls these unconscious processes *'simpletons'*. He says the unconscious mind is made up of myriads of automatons; simple processes that are responsible for automatically performing small groups of tasks. Similarly, Marvin Minsky (1986), an American Cognitive Scientist has labeled the unconscious mind a *'society of mind'*. By this he means that our unconscious mind consists largely of a society or population of relatively autonomous processes that communicate and interact with one another, much like members of society do with one another.

The insight that our mind is not unitary, not a single amorphous consciousness, is extremely important and useful. It explains why we often have conflicting parts and desires. Why we often act incongruently and undermine our own success. It's the reason why people can want and seek happiness and yet destroy this by succumbing to the very enemies of their happiness.

The nature of the brain and mind is that whenever we perform any behavior, we increase the probability that we will perform the behavior again. And through repetition of behavior, whether that behavior is an action, thought or feeling, we create a part of our brain/mind that automates the skill of the behavior. We create unconscious competence in a behavior and the part of our mind responsible for this skill operates automatically. It is a simpleton and automaton, often operating outside of conscious awareness.

And what applies to the brain in our head also applies to the brains in our heart and gut regions. As the field of *m*BIT shows, much of the intuitive intelligence of the heart and gut brains is processed out of our conscious awareness. And we form patterns and habits in how we communicate with and tune into the wisdom of our heart and gut and how they respond to the world. The gut and heart neural networks also exhibit learning, memory and neuro-plasticity. They are adaptive. So we can end up with unconscious competencies, habits and skills in the core competencies and prime functions of all our multiple brains (head, heart and gut).

So you need to be very careful of the thoughts, emotions and actions you take. Repeated behaviors generate '*parts*' in our unconscious mind; habits of success or failure. This is a vital and important understanding and we have incorporated it again and again in Journeys in this book.

Communicating with the Unconscious - Milton Patterns, Trance-formations and Artfully Guiding Language

Many of the NLP techniques were originally created by behavioral modeling of *'therapeutic wizards'* such as Milton Erickson, Virginia Satir and Fritz Perls (O'Connor & Seymour, 2011). These people were psychotherapists that could communicate with the unconscious minds of their clients and bring about lasting generative change.

One of these key set of NLP tools and distinctions is known as the Milton Model (or sometimes known as Milton Patterns). These linguistic and behavioral patterns were modeled by Richard Bandler and John Grinder, the co-developers of NLP, from Milton Erickson and are used to guide people into hypnotic trance. Milton was a noted American psychiatrist and medical hypnotherapist and was considered to be one of the best hypnosis practitioners in the world. He was a wizard at *artfully guiding* people into deeply generative trances to unlock new possibilities in their lives and bring about unconscious change.

You can read more about the Milton Model in one of Bandler and Grinder's wonderful books listed in the references section, such as Trance-formations (1981), or Patterns of the Hypnotic Techniques of Milton H. Erickson, Volumes 1 and 2 (1976, 1996).

The Milton model has three primary aspects: Building rapport with the person undergoing trance; Overloading and distracting the conscious mind so that unconscious communication can be more easily achieved, and; Allowing for ambiguity in artfully guiding the person to enable their own personal interpretation of the hypnotic communication.

A full explication of all of the Milton Patterns is beyond the scope of this Appendix. However, we will explore a summary of some of the key patterns with examples of how they are used:

Pacing Current Experience

In order to build rapport with the unconscious mind, Milton would make statements that matched the client's current phenomenological experience (e.g. "as you are hearing the sound of my voice..."). Statements that are easily verifiable in sensory experience to a person build a positive yes-set and trust and allow the person to continue to follow further commands and statements that are not verifiable.

Ambiguity

The ambiguity pattern is a key pattern for inducing trance, Milton used ambiguity to overload, distract and confuse his client's conscious mind and blur the boundaries of meaning allowing multiple meanings to be triggered across memory traces. There are four types of ambiguity patterns: Phonological Ambiguity, Punctuation Ambiguity, Syntactic Ambiguity and Scope Ambiguity. An example of phonological ambiguity is the use of the word 'here' which also can be heard unconsciously as 'hear'.

Conjunctions and causal linkages

Conjunctions such as 'and', 'as', 'then' etc. allow one thing to be linked to another at the unconscious level. This is simple form of linkage. Stronger forms of causal linkages are 'Implied Cause and Effect' and 'Direct Cause and Effect'. These cause and effect statements imply that one thing leads to or causes another. An example of using conjunctions and direct cause and effect would be: "And as you relax more deeply this allows you to begin to connect with your inner wisdom."

Embedded Commands

Embedded commands are commands that are part of a larger sentence. They are typically marked out using a subtle change of voice tonality or body language. The unconscious mind notices these changes and is influenced by the shorter command. An example of commanding the person's unconscious mind to connect with and 'find' them self would be *"And you can FIND YOURSELF drifting deeper now."*

Presuppositions

Presuppositions are linguistic assumptions that are implied in a sentence or statement. For the statement to be considered valid and true, the presupposition must unconsciously be accepted (e.g. *"and you can relax even more now"* which presupposes they are already relaxing.)

Selectional Restriction Violation

Selectional Restriction Violation is the attribution of intelligence, feelings or animation to inanimate objects. It is a confusion technique that in order to make sense of the statement, the unconscious applies the attribute or implication to the person them self (e.g. *"as you are sitting now on the meditative rock"* implies and encourages the person to become meditative.)

Double Binds

Creating the illusion of choice, such that no matter what the person does they are following what has been commanded or offered as the only range of choices (e.g. *"you can follow along with the Journey, or not."* Another example would be, *"You can keep your eyes open or shut, either way is right."*)

Metaphor

The use of metaphor can range from simple figures of speech, to allegories, stories and the use of mythical elements. It is used to create stories that operate on many levels and bypass the more critical functions of the conscious mind. As work in the field of Cognitive Linguistics has shown (Lakoff & Johnson, 1980), much of metaphor is deeply embodied. Thus to make sense of a metaphorical expression the unconscious mind connects with and evokes the embodied (autonomic, kinesthetic, heart, gut, pelvic etc.) intelligence and representation. This makes metaphor powerful for guiding new embodied forms of meaning and evoking intuitive wisdom. Stories, especially when combined with nested loops and deep layering can be very generative. An example of their use in a Guided Journey would be use of symbolic and metaphorical elements such as rainbows, mountains, deep pools etc.

Nested Loops and Layering

Nested Loops are the placing of one loop or story within another. – a story nested within a story. Loops or stories can be nested many layers deep. An example would be opening a loop or metaphor, part way through jumping into another story, when the second story is finished then returning at the end to the same first loop or story to complete it. Layering is where you literally layer in a story, message or metaphor or elements of these into another larger story. In essence it is a form of *'planting seeds'* and then metaphorically watering them to grow a much deeper acceptance at the unconscious level of an embedded message. The reason nested loops and layering work are because the unconscious mind can track many messages at once and finds and combines the separate threads together. Nested loops also work to nest the meaning of one message within another so that the two become associated together.

143

Sequential stories or messages, that are not nested, are much more difficult to get the patterning system of the unconscious mind to combine and associate together. Nested loops, which are often used in movies, songs and novels, provide a beautiful sense of completeness and delight when the loops are all closed one after the other and you find yourself returned to where you began with the first loop or story being completed.

Sensory Modalities and Submodalities

Each of us has patterns and preferences in how we utilize our five senses to *'make sense'* of the world. In context, some people may put more of their attention and neural capacity onto the visual component of their world, others on the auditory and yet others on the feeling or kinesthetic component. Trance can be easily evoked by taking someone from their *'normal'* sensory experience into an altered way (for them) of attending to their sensory world.

From an *m*BIT perspective, each of the brains has sensory channels that it utilizes and is optimized for. The gut for example is deeply involved in taste. The heart is linked to smell (notice how for heart-based romance we use beautiful smelling flowers, perfumes, etc.). The head of course evolved for tracking vision and sound, including speech. Action research in *m*BIT has uncovered that each of us also has a neural-syntax preference in how we attend to and use our multiple brains. Context dependent, some people prefer to use their heart first, others the gut, still others the head, and various combinations of these. So by using sensory predicates appropriately you can guide people into each of the senses and the corresponding embodied neural systems and thereby induce quite profound altered states.

Each sensory modality also has sub-components, which are known as *'submodalities.'* So submodalities are the finer details of the sensory representational systems. For example, for the visual system, submodalities include brightness, focus, color hue and density, distance, size etc. By evoking and influencing the submodalities of an experience you can deepen trance extensively (e.g. making things brighter, closer, stronger, deeper).

The Power of NLP and *m*BIT

As you can see from above, the models and insights from NLP and *m*BIT are incredibly synergistic and fit beautifully together. Each has its own power and benefits, and when used together within guided visualizations they produce an incredible set of tools for generative change and bringing the human spirit alive.

Acknowledgements and thanks

This book came into existence through a long and generative journey that started with NLP and more recently moved forward with the co-development of *m*BIT. Along the way, the Creative Journeys shared in this book were road-tested and action-researched with my beloved wife Fiona Soosalu. I can't thank her deeply enough for her wonderful support, encouragement and feedback.

I'd also like to acknowledge all those in the *m*BIT Community who provided feedback and action research. And in particular I'd like to express my deep, deep thanks and appreciation to *m*BIT Trainer and Master Coach, Christel Land, who so generously provided the beautiful artwork used on the cover and within the book and also thank her wonderful graphic artist, Shanaka Thisara, who created the beautiful imagery.

Of course, I'd also like to deeply thank my amazing parents who taught me what it means to share, love and make a difference to those you care about. Thank you, I love and appreciate you deeply and wondrously with all my heart.

Finally, I'd like to end this acknowledgement, as I started it by thanking my beloved Fiona for being such an important part of my life, you are a key and vital source in all my journeys and adventurings.

Legal stuff

As indicated at the front of this publication, the author and publisher have used their best efforts in preparing this book. This publication contains ideas, opinions, tips and techniques for improving wisdom, happiness and human performance. The materials are intended to provide helpful and useful material on the subjects addressed in the publication. The publisher and author do *not* provide or purport to provide you with any medical, health, psychological or professional advice or service or any other personal professional service. You should seek the advice of your own medical practitioner, health professional or other relevant competent professional before trying or using information, exercises or techniques described in this publication.

The publisher and author, jointly and severally, make no representations or warranties with respect to the accuracy, reliability, sufficiency or completeness of the contents of this publication and specifically disclaim any implied warranties or merchantability or fitness for any particular purpose. There are no warranties which extend beyond the descriptions contained in this paragraph. The accuracy and completeness of the information provided herein and the opinions stated herein are not guarantees, nor warranties to or towards the production of any particular result, and the advice and strategies contained herein may not be suitable for every individual.

You read this publication with the explicit understanding that neither the publisher, nor author shall be liable for any direct or indirect loss of profit or any other commercial damages, including but not limited to special, incidental, punitive, consequential or other damages. In reading or using any part or portion of this publication, you agree to not hold, nor attempt to hold the publisher or authors liable for any loss, liability, claim, demand, damage and all legal cost or other expenses arising whatsoever in connection with the use, misuse or inability to use the materials. In jurisdictions that exclude such limitations, liability is limited to the consideration paid by you for the right to view or use these materials, and/or the greatest extent permitted by law.

About the author

Grant Soosalu

Grant is an international Trainer, Leadership Consultant and Executive Coach with extensive backgrounds in Organizational Change, Training and Leadership Development. He has advanced degrees and certifications in Psychology, Positive Psychology, Applied Physics, Computer Engineering and System Development. He is a qualified Total Quality Management (TQM) Trainer, and has achieved Master Practitioner Certification in the behavioral sciences of Neuro Linguistic Programming (NLP) and Advanced Behavioral Modeling. More recently Grant was awarded a Graduate Coaching Diploma in the newly emerging field of Authentic Happiness Coaching.

Grant has wide ranging expertise and experience in the educational sector as a Lecturer, Coach, Training Developer and Facilitator. He also has extensive backgrounds in Business Development, Senior Technical Consulting and Project Management. Grant provides coaching and mentoring to CEO's and Senior Executives around the world.

Grant is the co-developer of the exciting new field of *m*BIT (multiple Brain Integration Techniques) and has published articles and papers in leading International Journals, in the fields of Coaching, Leadership, Philosophy, Psychotherapy, Social Sciences, Applied Physics and NLP.

References and resources

References

Adams FM and Osgood CE, A Cross-Cultural Study of the Affective Meanings of Color. Journal of Cross-Cultural Psychology, June 1, 1973. Volume: 4 issue: 2, page(s): 135-156.

Armour J, (2007). The little brain on the heart. Cleveland Clinic Journal of Medicine, 74, S48-S51.

Aslam MM, Are You Selling the Right Colour? A Cross-cultural Review of Colour as a Marketing Cue. Journal of Marketing Communications. (2006). 12 (1): 15–30.

Atchley RA, Strayer DL and Atchley P, Creativity in the Wild: Improving Creative Reasoning through Immersion in Natural Settings. PLoS ONE 7(12): e51474. (2012).

Bandler R and Grinder J, (1976). Patterns of the Hypnotic Techniques of Milton H. Erickson, M.D. Volume 1. Cupertino, CA :Meta Publications. ISBN 0-916990-01-X.

Bandler R, DeLozier J and Grinder J, (1996). Patterns of the Hypnotic Techniques of Milton H. Erickson, M.D. Volume 2. Cupertino, CA : Metamorphous Press. ISBN 978-1555520533.

Bargh JA and Morsella E. The Unconscious Mind. *Perspect Psychol Sci*. 2008;3(1):73-9.

Beissner F, Meissner K, Bär KJ and Napadow V, The Autonomic Brain: An Activation Likelihood Estimation Meta-Analysis for

Central Processing of Autonomic Function. J Neurosci. 2013 Jun 19; 33(25): 10503–10511.

Bernardi L, Sleight P, Bandinelli G, Cencetti S, Fattorini L, Wdowczyc-Szulc J and Lagi A, Effect of rosary prayer and yoga mantras on autonomic cardiovascular rhythms: comparative study. BMJ. 2001 Dec 22; 323(7327): 1446–1449.

Bernston G, Sarter M and Cacioppo J, (2003). Ascending visceral regulation of cortical affective information processing. European Journal of Neuroscience, 18(8), 2103-2109.

Blomhoff S, Spetalen S, Jacobsen MB, Vatn M and Malt UF, Intestinal reactivity to words with emotional content and brain information processing in irritable bowel syndrome. Dig Dis Sci. 2000 Jun;45(6):1160-5.

Brown JD and Mankowski TA, (1993). Self-esteem, mood, and self-evaluation: Changes in mood and the way you see you. Journal of Personality and Social Psychology, 64(3), 421-430.

Bourn J, Color Meaning: Meaning of The Color Blue. BournCreative, January 15, 2011.

Campbell J, The Power of Myth. New York: Anchor. (1991). ISBN 9780385418867.

Cascio CN, O'Donnell MB, Tinney FJ, Lieberman MD, Taylor SE, Strecher VJ and Falk EB, Self-affirmation activates brain systems associated with self-related processing and reward and is reinforced by future orientation. Soc Cogn Affect Neurosci. 2016 Apr; 11(4): 621–629.

Cohen GL and Sherman DK, The psychology of change: self-affirmation and social psychological intervention. Annu Rev Psychol. 2014;65:333-71.

Cooper JC, An Illustrated Encyclopaedia of Traditional Symbols. London: Thames and Hudson, 1978.

Coss RG, Ruff S and Simms T, All That Glistens: II. The Effects of Reflective Surface Finishes on the Mouthing Activity of Infants and Toddlers, (2003), Ecological Psychology, 15:3, 197-213.

Craig A, (2014). How do you feel?: An interoceptive Moment with your Neurobiological Self. New Jersey: Princeton University Press.

Creswell D, Dutcher JM, Klein WMP, Harris PR and Levine JM, Self-Affirmation Improves Problem-Solving under Stress J. PLOS ONE | www.plosone.org. 1 May 2013, Volume 8; Issue 5.

Critchley H, (2015). Interoception, Emotion and Self: How the Heart Gates Feelings and Perceptions. Retrieved from http://www.rotman.uwo.ca/events-2/hugo-critchley-interocpetion-emotion-and-self/

De Bortoli M and Maroto J, Colours Across Cultures, in the Proceedings of the European Languages and the Implementation of Communication and Information Technologies (Elicit) conference. University of Paisley. 2001.

Elliot AJ, Color and psychological functioning: a review of theoretical and empirical work. Front Psychol. 2015; 6: 368.

Epton T, Harris PR, Kane R, van Koningsbruggen GM and Sheeran, P, The impact of self-affirmation on health-behavior change: A meta-analysis. Health Psychology, Vol 34(3), Mar 2015, 187-196.

Erickson M, Hypnosis Gives You a Favorable Climate in which to Work. Youtube Video. Filmed in 1979, and published by Jane Parsons-Fein, 14 Oct 2013 https://www.youtube.com/watch?v=g172y9KIu6Y.

Fallon B, A(blue)nt: Beyond the Symbology of the Colour Blue. Literature & Aesthetics 24 (2) December 2014.

Frecska E, Levente M and Wesselman H, The soul cluster: Reconsideration of a millennia old concept. February 2011. World Futures The Journal of General Evolution 67:132-153.

Fromm E and Shor RE (2009). Hypnosis: Developments in Research and New Perspectives. Rutgers. ISBN 978-0-202-36262-5.

Gawain, S. (1978). *Creative Visualization*. Mill Valley, CA: New World Library.

Gershon M, (1999). The Second Brain - A Groundbreaking New Understanding of Nervous Disorders of the Stomach and Intestine. New York, NY: Harper Perennial.

Grinder J and Bandler R, (1981). Trance-formations: Neuro-Linguistic Programming and the Structure of Hypnosis. Real People Press. ISBN 978-0911226232.

Guéguen N & Stefan J, "Green Altruism": Short Immersion in Natural Green Environments and Helping Behavior. Environment and Behavior. (2016). 48(2), 324–342.

Haynes D, The Symbolism and Significance of the Butterfly in Ancient Egypt. MP diss., Arts & Social Sciences at Stellenbosch University Stellenbosch University, 2013.

Holzer P, (2017). Interoception and Gut Feelings: Unconscious Body Signals' Impact on Brain Function, Behavior and Belief Processes. In O. L. Angel H (Ed.), Process of Believing: The Acquisition, Maintenance, and Change in Creditions. Basel, Switzerland: Springer.

Holzer P, Schicho R, Holzer-Petsche U and Lippe, I, (2001). The gut as a neurological organ. Wein Klin Wochenscher, 113(17-18), 647-660.

Howards S and Crandall MW, (2007) Post TraumaEc Stress Disorder. Washington Academy of Sciences, Washington, D. C 93(4):1.

Howell AJ, Dopko RL, Passmore HA and Buro K, Nature connectedness: Associations with well-being and mindfulness. Personality and Individual Differences, Volume 51, Issue 2, July 2011, Pages 166-171.

Innes KE, Selfe TK, Kandati S, Wen S and Huysmans Z, Effects of Mantra Meditation versus Music Listening on Knee Pain, Function, and Related Outcomes in Older Adults with Knee Osteoarthritis: An Exploratory Randomized Clinical Trial (RCT). Evidence-Based

Complementary and Alternative Medicine, Volume 2018, Article ID 7683897, 19 pages.

Iyilikci O, Aydin E and Canbeyli R, Blue but not red light stimulation in the dark has antidepressant effect in behavioral despair. Behav Brain Res. 2009 Oct 12;203(1):65-8.

Jacobs KW and Suess JF, Effects of four psychological primary colors on anxiety state. Perceptual and Motor Skills (1975) 41(1):207-10.

Jiang H, White MP, Greicius MD, Waelde LC and Spiegel D, Brain Activity and Functional Connectivity Associated with Hypnosis. Cerebral Cortex, Volume 27, Issue 8, 1 August 2017, Pages 4083–4093.

Jung CG and Franz Mv, *Man and his symbols*. New York: Dell. 1968.

Kalyani BG, Venkatasubramanian G, Arasappa R et al., Neurohemodynamic correlates of 'OM' chanting: A pilot functional magnetic resonance imaging study. Int J Yoga. 2011 Jan-Jun; 4(1): 3–6.

Kaya N and Epps HH. Color-emotion association: Past experience and personal preference. The University of Georgia, Department of Textiles, Merchandising, and Interiors, 2004.

Kjellgren A and Buhrkall H, A comparison of the restorative effect of a natural environment with that of a simulated natural environment. Journal of Environmental Psychology, Volume 30, Issue 4, December 2010, Pages 464-472.

Kodeeswara Prabu P and Subhash J, Guided Imagery Therapy,IOSR Journal of Nursing and Health Science (IOSR-JNHS), Volume 4, Issue 5 Ver. III (Sep.- Oct. 2015), PP 56-58.

Korpela KM, Ylén M, Tyrväinen L and Silvennoinen H, Favorite green, waterside and urban environments, restorative experiences and perceived health in Finland. Health Promot Int. 2010 Jun;25(2):200-9.

Krakov SV, Color Vision and the Autonomic Nervous System. Journal of the Optical Society of America, June, 1942.

Kutchma TM, The Effects of Room Color on Stress Perception: Red versus Green Environments. Journal of Undergraduate Research at Minnesota State University, Mankato: Vol. 3, Article 3, 2003.

Lakoff G and Johnson M, Metaphors We Live By. Chicago: Chicago UP, 1980.

Lee JR, Raymond L and Fraser AB, The Rainbow Bridge: Rainbows in Art, Myth, and Science, Preface, p. viii, Penn State Press, 2001, ISBN 9780271019772.

Li X, Chen L, Ma R, Wang H, Wan L, Wang Y, Bu J, Hong W, Lv W, Vollstädt-Klein S, Yang Y and Zhang X, The top-down regulation from the prefrontal cortex to insula via hypnotic aversion suggestions reduces smoking craving. Hum Brain Mapp. 2018 Nov 22.

Lindquist KA, Satpute AB and Gendronc M, Does language do more than communicate emotion? Curr Dir Psychol Sci. 2015 Apr 1; 24(2): 99–108.

Litscher D, Wang L, Gaischek I and Litscher G, The Influence of New Colored Light Stimulation Methods on Heart Rate Variability, Temperature, and Well-Being: Results of a Pilot Study in Humans. Evid Based Complement Alternat Med. 2013; 2013: 674183.

Longe O, Maratos FA, Gilbert P, Evans G, Volker F, Rockliff H and Rippo G, Having a word with yourself: Neural correlates of self-criticism and self-reassurance. NeuroImage 49 (2010) 1849–1856.

Madden TJ, Hewett K and Roth MS, Managing Images in Different Cultures: A Cross-National Study of Color Meanings and Preferences, Journal of International Marketing, Vol. 8, No. 4, USA, 2000, pp. 90-107.

Malhotra V, Garg R, Dhar U, Goel N, Tripathy Y, Jaan I, Goyal S and Arora S, Mantra, music and reaction times: A study of its applied aspects. International Journal of Medical Research & Health Sciences 2014, Volume 3, Issue 4, pp. 825-828.

Mayer E, Gut feelings: the emerging biology of gut-brain communication. Nat Rev Neurosci., 12(8), (2011), 453-466.

McCormack F, Mind games. Scholastic Scope, Vol. 54, Iss. 10, New York: Jan 23, 2006.

Meares A, A System of Medical Hypnosis, Julian Press, (New York), 1960.

Meares A, Relief Without Drugs: The Self-Management of Tension, Anxiety and Pain, Fontana, (Sydney), 1970.

Meares A, Strange Places and Simple Truths. London : Fontana, 1973.

Mehta R and Zhu R, Blue or Red? Exploring the Effect of Color on Cognitive Task Performances. Science 27 Feb 2009: Vol. 323, Issue 5918, pp. 1226-1229.

Micozzi, M. Fundamentals of Complementary and Integrative Medicine, 3rd Ed. St. Louis: Elsevier. 2006.

Minsky M, The Society of Mind. 1986. New York: Simon & Schuster. ISBN 0-671-60740-5.

Mravec B and Hulin I, Does vagus nerve constitute a self-organization complexity or a "hidden network"? Bratisl Lek Listy. 2006; 107(1-2): 3-8.

Myriam V. Thoma, Roberto La Marca, Rebecca Brönnimann, Linda Finkel, Ulrike Ehlert and Urs M. Nater,The Effect of Music on the Human Stress Response. PLoS One. 2013; 8(8): e70156.

Naidu KL, Mohan Rao P, Kumar Goothy SS, et al., Beneficial effects of 12-week OM chanting on memory in school children. World Journal of Pharmaceutical Sciences 2(12):1969-1971 January 2014.

Naparstek B, Criteria on Indications and Contraindications, Desired Outcomes & Delivery of Guided Imagery and Mindfulness Audio Programs, October 18, 2016.

Nichols WJ, Blue Mind: The Surprising Science That Shows How Being Near, In, On, or Under Water Can Make You Happier, Healthier, More Connected, and Better at What You Do. Little, Brown & Company. New York, NY, 2015.

Oakley DA and Halligan PW, Hypnotic suggestion and cognitive neuroscience. Trends in Cognitive Sciences (2009) Vol.13 No.6, pp.264-270.

O'Connor J and Seymour J, Introducing NLP. Conari Press; Revised edition (2011). ISBN: 978-1573244985.

Ohtsuki M, A Cognitive Linguistic Study of Colour Symbolism. Volume 5 of Contributions towards research and education of language, ISSN 1342-615X, Institute for the Research and Education of Language, Daito-Bunka University, 2000.

Olesen J, Color Symbolism in Chinese Culture: What do Traditional Chinese Colors Mean? Online: color-meanings.com, 2018.

Ornstein R, The Evolution of Consciousness. Prentice-Hall US, 1991.

Park BJ, Tsunetsugu Y, Kasetani T, Kagawa T and Miyazaki Y, The physiological effects of Shinrin-yoku (taking in the forest atmosphere or forest bathing): evidence from field experiments in 24 forests across Japan. Environ Health Prev Med. 2010 Jan; 15(1): 18–26.

Park G and Thayer J, (2014). From the heart to the mind: cardiac vagal tone modulates top-down and bottom-up visual perception and attention to emotional stimuli. Front. Psychol., 5, 278.

Pauly K, Finkelmeyer A, Schneider F and Habel U, The neural correlates of positive self-evaluation and self-related memory. Soc Cogn Affect Neurosci. 2013 Dec; 8(8): 878–886.

Pérez-Lloret S, Diez J, Domé MN, Delvenne AA, Braidot N, Cardinali DP, Vigo DE. Effects of different "relaxing" music styles on the autonomic nervous system. Noise Health 2014;16:279-84.

Philine S. Harris, Peter R. Harris and Eleanor M. Self-affirmation improves performance on tasks related to executive functioning Journal of Experimental Social Psychology 70 (2017) 281–285.

Pilorz V, Tam SKE, Hughes S, Pothecary CA, Jagannath A, Hankins MW, et al. (2016) Melanopsin Regulates Both Sleep-Promoting and Arousal-Promoting Responses to Light. PLoS Biol 14(6): e1002482.

Porges SW, The Polyvagal Theory - Neurophysiological Foundations of Emotions, Attachment, Communication, and Self-regulation, Norton & Company, 2011.

Pradhan B and Godse Derle S,Comparison of effect of Gayatri Mantra and Poem Chanting on Digit Letter Substitution Task. Anc Sci Life. 2012 Oct-Dec; 32(2): 89–92.

Protas A, Brown G, Smith J and Jaffe E, Disctionary of Symbolism, University of Michigan, 2001.

Roberts J, What Colors Mean in Other Cultures. Huffpost Life, SmarterTravel Contributor, Online, January 26, 2017.

Robinson B, (1907). The abdominal and pelvic brain with autonomic visceral ganglia. Chicago,Illinois: Franz Betz Hammond Ind.

Roque MÀ, Birds: Metaphor of the Soul. Quaderns de la Mediterrània, 2010 12:96 - 108.

Ross MJ, Guthrie P, Dumont JC, The impact of modulated, colored light on the autonomic nervous system. Adv Mind Body Med. 2013 Fall; 27(4):7-16.

Rossman M, Holistic Primary Care News, Vol. 7, No. 4. Winter, 2006.

Saxbe DE, Yang XF, Borofsky LA and Immordino-Yang MH, The embodiment of emotion: language use during the feeling of social emotions predicts cortical somatosensory activity. Soc Cogn Affect Neurosci. 2013 Oct;8(7):806-12.

Scaglione R and Cummins W, Karate of Okinawa: Building Warrior Spirit, Tuttle Publishing, 1993, ISBN 096264840X.

Schmeichel BJ and Vohs K, Self-affirmation and self-control: Affirming core values counteracts ego depletion Journal of Personality and Social Psychology, 96 (4) (2009), pp. 770-782.

Schwartz AE, Guided Imagery for Groups: Fifty Visualizations that Promote Relaxation, Problem-solving, Creativity, and Well-being. Abe Books, 1995.

Shackell, E. M., and Standing, L. G. (2007). Mind over matter: mental training increases physical strength. North Am. J. Psychol. 9, 189–200.

Soosalu G and Oka M, (2012). mBraining: Using your multiple brains to do cool stuff. Timebinding Publications.

Telles S, Nagarathna R and Nagendra HR, Autonomic changes during "OM" meditation. Indian J Physiol Pharmacol. 1995 Oct;39(4):418-20.

Telles S, Nagarathna R and Nagendra HR, Autonomic changes while mentally repeating two syllables--one meaningful and the other neutral. Indian J Physiol Pharmacol. 1998 Jan;42(1):57-63.

Thayer J, (2007). What the heart says to the brain (and vice versa) and why we should listen. Psychological Topics, 16(2), 241-250.

Ulrich RS, View through a window may influence recovery from surgery. Science 27 Apr 1984: Vol. 224, Issue 4647, pp. 420-421.

Vianna EP, Naqvi N, Bechara A, and Tranel D, Does vivid emotional imagery depend on body signals? Int J Psychophysiol. 2009 Apr;72(1):46-50.

Völker S and Kistemann T, The impact of blue space on human health and well-being - Salutogenetic health effects of inland surface waters: a review. Int J Hyg Environ Health. 2011 Nov;214(6):449-60.

Völker S and Kistemann T, "I'm always entirely happy when I'm here!" Urban blue enhancing human health and well-being in Cologne and Düsseldorf, Germany. Soc Sci Med. 2013 Feb;78:113-24.

Waitley D, The Psychology of Winning. Brolga Publishing, 2002.

Weigensberg, M.J., Lane, C.J., Wright, T., & Goran, M.I. (2009). Acute Effects of Stress-Reduction Interactive Guided Imagery(SM) on Salivary Cortisol in Overweight Latino Adolescents. Journal of alternative and complementary medicine, 15(3), 297-303.

Weil A, Guided Imagery Therapy, Accessed online Nov 2018. https://www.drweil.com/health-wellness/balanced-living/wellness-therapies/guided-imagery-therapy/

Weydert JA, Shapiro DE, Acra SA, Monheim CJ, Chambers AS and Ball TM, Evaluation of guided imagery as treatment for recurrent abdominal pain in children: a randomized controlled trial. BMC Pediatrics, 2006 6:29.

Wheeler BW, White M, Stahl-Timmins W and Depledge MH, Does living by the coast improve health and wellbeing? Health & Place, 2012.

White MP, Alcock I, Wheeler BW and Depledge MH, Coastal proximity, health and well-being: Results from a longitudinal panel survey. Health & Place Volume 23, September 2013, Pages 97-103.

White MP, Pahl S, Ashbullby K, Herbert S and Depledge MH, Feelings of restoration from recent nature visits. Journal of Environmental Psychology, Volume 35, September 2013, Pages 40-51.

White, MP, Pahl S, Wheeler BW, Fleming LEF and Depledge MH, The 'Blue Gym': What Can Blue Space Do for You and What Can You Do for Blue Space? Journal of the Marine Biological Association of the United Kingdom 96.1 (2016): 5-12.

Wolf N, Vagina: A New Biography, Dec 2013. New York, New York: Ecco. ISBN 9780061989162.

Yang Y, Fairbairn C and Cohn JF, Detecting Depression Severity from Vocal Prosody, IEEE Trans Affect Comput. 2013 Apr-Jun; 4(2): 142–150.

Yao WX, Ranganathan VK, Allexandre D, Siemionow V and Yue GH, Kinesthetic imagery training of forceful muscle contractions increases brain signal and muscle strength. Front. Hum. Neurosci., 26 September 2013.

Additional Resources

Additional resources and information on the new field of multiple Brain Integration Techniques (*m*BIT), including free articles, whitepapers, exercises and mp3's can be found at:

www.mbraining.com

Information on Grant's other books, *'Avoiding the Enemies to HAPPINESS'* and *'Loving your Life'* can be found at:

www.avoidingtheenemies.com

and

www.lyl-book.com

And if you'd like to read Grant's Life Enhancing blog, go to:

enhancingmylife.blogspot.com

Made in the USA
Columbia, SC
16 October 2022

69535198R00100